GRAND RAPIDS
FOOD

GRAND RAPIDS
FOOD

A CULINARY REVOLUTION

LISA ROSE STARNER

AMERICAN PALATE

Published by American Palate
A Division of The History Press
Charleston, SC 29403
www.historypress.net

All chapter heading art courtesy of the artist, Alynn Guerra.

First published 2013

Manufactured in the United States

ISBN 978.1.60949.731.6

Library of Congress CIP data applied for.

Notice: The information in this book is true and complete to the best of
our knowledge. It is offered without guarantee on the part of the author or
The History Press. The author and The History Press disclaim all liability in
connection with the use of this book.

To John Arnold (1950–2012), who taught me to be passionate in my beliefs, resolute in my actions and to always offer compassion along the way.

Contents

Acknowledgements

It would suffice to say that there are many thanks due to the many people who assisted me in the creation of this book. First and foremost, I am grateful for the local food community in which I work. I sought out to include the voices of a variety of people who are rolling up their sleeves and building this movement from scratch. There are many other stories to be told, many other voices to be heard and successes to be shared. This is only a snippet—a snapshot of how we are growing and learning how to grow together.

I am grateful to everyone that graciously offered me their time in talking about their work. As a participant in this movement, this book also afforded me a good opportunity to "check in" and see how we are doing as a whole. To be sure, there is a lot of work to be done. But these conversations gave me hope for the future of my city.

As for telling the stories, I have to admit that it was a difficult process. I assembled bits and pieces at a time and struggled to weave them together over the course of the past year. I have to thank my friend and hyperlocal editor Holly Bechiri at the *Rapidian*, who helped me take these pieces and weave them together with a golden thread. Holly consistently had my back when it came to needing a second set of eyes, creative brain power or simply someone with whom to just share a plate of restaurant macaroni and cheese when the stress just got to be too much. She was the only person I really trusted to review my copy—such soul-baring work for a new writer. Holly was kind but firm with her red pen, and I cannot express my gratitude enough. And to my childhood English teachers—Mrs. VanderStelt, Mrs.

Holden and Mrs. Millard—thank you for teaching me the value of that red pen and providing me with foundational writing skills. Please know that I will pass on the mentorship to other young writers wishing to use the pen as a tool for social change.

It cannot go without mention the names of many artists and photographers that came to my aid to help me tell these stories visually. I had a great time interacting with several of the photographers on shoots for this book, and I learned that the dynamics within the art community are very similar to those in the food community. We could learn a lot from each other. Food for thought.

Thanks go out to these artists, photographers and colleagues (in no particular order) for their contribution of imagery to illustrate the narrative of this book: Teresa Zbiciak, Stephanie Harding, Chad Morton, David McGowan, Jonathan Stoner, Greg Gilmore, The Image Shoppe, Lynette Gram, Michelle Smith, Grand Rapids Public Library Archival Department, MLive, West Michigan Academy of Environmental Science, Taylor Voss, Baxter Community Center, Slow Food West Michigan, Spectrum Health, YMCA of Greater Grand Rapids, Jeff Hill, Terry Johnston, Andy Sietsema, Ryan Pavlovich, Rick and Brenda Beerhorst, Alynn Guerra, Andy and Elizabeth deBraber, Andy Dragt, Shane Folkertsma, Ahavas Israel, Temple Emanuel, Feeding America West Michigan, George Aquino, John Russo, Adam Bird, the Fulton Street Farmers' Market, Grand Action, Founders Brewing Co., Barfly Ventures and the Lubbers Family Farm.

I must also give a huge thanks to all my friends and family who tolerated my kvetching about the writing process. Even after several of my self-imposed deadlines passed, I am glad they all still had hope that I would finish this piece and continued to cheer me on. And if they actually had lost hope and began to doubt I'd ever finish, well, at least they were gracious enough to never say so to my face. Specifically, a shout-out goes to Jeff Hill, who kept on me to finish the manuscript, and to Roberta F. King, whose own journey to publish her memoir kept me inspired to keep writing—so we could go running. And to Lorissa MacAllister, thank you, dear woman, for always believing in my talents. I love you like a sister.

Gratitude must also be expressed to my husband, who has learned over our past ten years together to not flinch at my manic work habits. Seth, I'm always grateful for your steadfast support of all my endeavors.

A special mention goes to my departed friend Phil Chafee for his support of this book. When I found myself with a contract and no agent, Phil took me on as a client and had my back as great legal counsel. Sadly, Phil passed away unexpectedly just a few days after I received my signed contract. Upon learning of his graceful departure from this earth, the first thing that I said out loud was, "Dammit Phil, you never sent me your bill for your hours!" It's funny, in the whole cosmic scheme of things, I don't think he really ever intended on sending me a bill. But that was Phil—he always worked straight from the heart. Dear Phil, you know I'll pay your love forward. We all miss you, man.

Finally, I must thank Joe Gartrell at The History Press for taking a risk on my talents as a new author. All he knew of me when he offered me a book contract was what he saw on social media, and for that I am humbled, grateful and slightly shocked that my unedited social media persona didn't scare him off. I am equally grateful that he didn't replace me with another author when it took me twice as long than I anticipated to complete this project. I do hope he feels the final product was worth the wait.

In the end, I offer this work in honor of the efforts of those working hard to make change in our local food system. I hope that readers will gain a fresh perspective on the local food movement in Grand Rapids and will be inspired to become part of this powerful force to help change our community one fork at a time! It is very important that we develop an economy that values local food production, because ultimately, our health, environment and economy all depend on it. So pick up your fork and join the movement.

—LISA ROSE STARNER, 2013

Prologue

THE TREEHOUSE COMMUNITY GARDEN

The Treehouse Community Garden is a sanctuary for those who live in and around this southeast-side neighborhood. Neighbors stroll by in the morning sunshine while birds practice their chirping. "Beautiful garden," they call from the street. "You are welcome to come in and visit anytime," Amy Bowditch calls back.[1]

A woman enters the garden, and Amy breaks away to talk with her. "There's seven of us living together who made this space so that neighborhood families could have a place to grow vegetables in this community garden," she says. Small talk ensues. "What happened to the rain?" the woman asks. "We were just about to do our rain dance," laughs Amy.

They talk about using beet tops and chard greens and sautéing them for scrambled eggs. "Awesome—I never knew that you could eat beet tops!" the woman exclaims. "And what is this? Eggplant? Wow. I learned something new this morning. Thanks ladies, you all have a good day. Thanks for inviting me."

As the woman leaves the garden, Amy smiles. "Yea, so this is us—this is what we do," she says. "We enjoy it. It's rewarding. Just growing stuff is rewarding. Being here, interacting with neighbors, being available and learning about neighbors and their cultures. One family is from Mexico, another from Puerto Rico."

The neighborhood that Amy Bowditch is rooted in is known as the Baxter neighborhood, located on the city's southeast side. The garden, located on Logan Avenue Southeast, has been historically categorized as one of the most hardcore urban environments in the city of Grand Rapids. For several decades, residents like Bowditch have worked to take back control of the fate of the neighborhood and those who live there. Bowditch and her group, the Treehouse Community Gardeners, were provided with a house and some land, a little under an acre, on which they could garden. The property is owned and managed by the Inner City Christian Federation (ICCF), a nonprofit organization that helps with the redevelopment and rental of property within the inner city. ICCF arranged a long-term lease with the resident gardeners to allow them to pursue their work. Bowditch notes, "As far as I can tell, they have no plans for kicking us out. ICCF owns a lot of property here on Logan Avenue. They own many of these properties—a few are foreclosed. Property values are so low that they are having a hard time getting families to want to move here."

The Treehouse Community Garden wasn't built by any single person; it was a group effort. Not only that, but the garden received very generous donations from community businesses. From the concrete slab to the lumber, the TreeHouse Community Garden was created from the effort and input of many.

Amy and her housemates have been residents of this neighborhood for nearly two years, living in an intentional community in the Baxter neighborhood. She recalls:

There were several of us, and we more or less started wanting to live together and share resources—we wanted to work toward being more sustainable. We started forming relationships with the neighbors—having them over for dinner, watching each other's kids. Saturday mornings after breakfast, we would walk around the neighborhood to clean up the streets. All we were cleaning up were Cheetos bags and Bug Juice bottles…endless amounts of just disgusting trash. It made me think, "What are these kids eating?" Then, one summer day, I was eating a snack on the porch, and the neighborhood kids asked to have some. They were so hungry. Knowing what I know about poverty, I know these kids aren't eating the foods they need to be eating. So I said, "Wait a minute," went into the house and brought some more food out. I didn't feel like it was enough to just hand these kids food; I needed to explain to them the system that is set in place and how they eat this food that isn't healthy for them, which is why they are hungry all the time. Maybe it will click when they are older and they are able to make these choices for their own families. We see kids with diabetes, overweight kids in wheelchairs who can barely function, kids who are tired and cannot focus—these kids are lacking. Some of these kids have parents who even smoke crack. I always hear, "We ran out of food stamps because mom had to sell them all." It's sad—it's hard for me to listen to some of these stories.

In a soft, determined voice, Amy sounds defeated yet resolute in the purpose behind the garden. "People are skeptical of what our motives are. Can you blame them? I would be skeptical, too. But I live here. They recognize us—they see us. All we want to do is grow food."

Chapter 1

The Grand Rapids
Food Revolution

Our global food system is fraught with social, economic and environmental disparity and brokenness. Cities have become detached from local farms and food resources. Local farms have been separated from the urban communities, and they struggle to find alternative ways to sell their produce locally rather than corporately over long distances.

But all hope is not lost. In communities and cities all across the United States, citizens are looking to reclaim their food systems. Eaters are looking to reconnect with their growers. Neighborhoods are building farm markets, and neighbors are building gardens. Communities are looking for ways to make sure those without food can eat. Farmers are growing their operations with the intention to care for the land that is sustaining the crops and offering a fair work environment for the people in the fields. Restaurants are featuring these wares from the earth on their menus.

Michigan farmers are trying to remain competitive in a global agricultural market, and many small farmers are re-creating the food system so that they may have economically viable small-scale production farms within local markets.

Along with the beauty of sandy beaches, Lake Michigan sunsets, pristine fields and forests, Michigan's rich soils and microclimates allow for a wide range of agricultural crops to grow throughout the state, resulting in a diversity of crops second only to California. Rich in agricultural history, the Greater Grand Rapids area has always had immediate access to fresh, local foods. In the past fifteen years, there has been an intentional focus within the food community to come together, discuss and find solutions to the pressing issues that are central to what we eat.

This is more than a foodie movement; it is a cultural revolution. Grand Rapids has an army of food activists working to increase access to fresh foods within the urban community through a myriad of channels, including community gardens, urban farms, food cooperatives and a more effective pantry system. Citizens have taken up shovels to clear grass and concrete and build gardens. When policy gets in the way, citizens continue to appear at policy meetings to help coax our leaders to make changes. And in the face of a recession that is wiping out jobs and driving a high rise in foreclosures, the local food system keeps growing and, in turn, grows our local economy.

Grand Rapids citizens are choosing local food for a multitude of reasons—for health, for a stronger economy, for social justice. Many also choose local food as a strategy to protect our natural resources, to ensure fair wages for farmers and their workers, to solve food insecurity and simply to be healthy. Local citizens are choosing local food as a solution to the most pressing questions of our generation's time. "A strong local food economy is essential to creating a vibrant, sustainable West Michigan,"[2] says Elissa Sangalli Hillary, director of Local First. Local First, originally incorporated as BALLE, or the Business Alliance for Local Living Economies, was created by local Grand Rapids business leaders to raise awareness and build Grand Rapids' local economy. The group places a particular focus on the local food economy. Hillary continues:

> As the largest sector of our economy, agriculture provides good jobs and keeps wealth within our community. Small- and medium-scale family farms protect our environment and provide healthy nourishment for local eaters. In addition, our grocers, restaurateurs and culinary artisans contribute greatly to our culture. We know that if we shift just one in ten dollars to local businesses, we can create 1,600 jobs in Kent County alone. This is a huge number, and one of the easiest ways to do this is by redirecting where individuals are spending their money on food. We all have to eat, and by consciously making decisions about where your food comes from, you can literally change and build the economy around you.

As part of their "Edible Education" and outreach, Slow Food seeks to connect people to traditional food ways as means to preserve the art of the table. Here, a participant learns about harvesting and preparing Michigan wild rice. *Photo courtesy of Slow Food West Michigan.*

Choosing local food builds local economies and strengthens and preserves local food cultures. Slow Food, a food movement that originated in Italy and urges us to "eat slow" in an effort to learn about and preserve traditional food ways, has worked diligently to support the food movements across the world. In Grand Rapids, a chapter of Slow Food, Slow Food West Michigan, frequently offers unique educational opportunities for eaters to reconnect with local food traditions. As part of its Edible Education program, Slow Food West Michigan offers farm-to-table dinners and hands-on demonstrations as ways to catalyze conversations about local food diversity, quality and access. Slow Food West Michigan also gives public recognition of food sustainability efforts by local restaurants, farmers, food artisans, distributors, breweries and markets with its "Snail of Approval."

Efforts like these, and the stories that follow center on people and organizations trying to make a local difference and create a local food system that is good, fair, affordable and green.

This isn't a story about saving the world through local food, though in the end, the actions may in fact be the answers. This is a story about the process of creating new innovations in the food community, whether it's increasing access to good food for local neighborhoods or new businesses or creating a new community garden for the neighborhood. The efforts are many, and together we are working toward a community that will ensure access to food that is healthful, affordable, socially just and grown in a sustainable way for our city.

Chapter 2

Designing Place: Planning for Diversity in the Urban Garden

Vibrancy is kind of like porn—you know it when you see it. The best neighborhoods in the best cities in the world have great attractions like bars, restaurants, galleries, etc., but they also have pharmacies, hardware stores, book shops, and non-trendy cafes that serve the people who live there—both the cool and uncool—whose mere existence and use of the neighborhood is what makes it truly vibrant.[3]
—Tyler Dornbos

Access to good food affects health and one's ability to learn, thrive and survive. It has economic implications and is part of our collective social fabric. A good food system is a key facet to having quality of life. Grand Rapids city planner Suzanne Schultz knows this. City planner for nearly thirteen years, Suzanne Schultz has had a lot to do with the sustainable growth and direction of Grand Rapids in the past decade. Schultz was at the helm directing the creation of the Grand Rapids master plan and guiding documents that brought back the city's natural resources and placed them at the forefront of the city's planning and design. Her unending commitment to engage citizens in creative participatory planning processes resulted in a plan for the city that (un)paved the way for greening parks, bike lanes and care for our watersheds. She has truly set the tone for an overall more vibrant approach to the city's planning.

Schultz lacks much of the hubris that one might expect from a high-level city staffer and attributes much of the success of the city's master plan to the engagement and dedication of her fellow Grand Rapidians. "Citizens of Grand Rapids are not satisfied with the status quo," she says. "When we do compare ourselves to other cities, we always compare ourselves to the bigger cities. We always go big, never comparing ourselves to similar cities like Rochester. No—we compare ourselves to Chicago. We don't care about Rochester—we want Chicago. We are yearning to be more as a city—status quo isn't good enough."[4]

Schultz understands the complexity within the food systems of larger cities. For her, planning good food access throughout the city includes working with citizens and organizations to develop community gardens and establish neighborhood farmers' markets, supporting the growing of backyard gardens and creating zoning for thriving food businesses. Having farmland in nearby areas is also part of the equation.

Prior to her post as an urban city planner, Schultz spent a great deal of time in township planning in the rural areas of Algoma, Courtland and Howard City. She saw firsthand the number of farms phasing out because of the retirement of aging farmers. It disturbed Schultz that the township, county and state governments weren't doing more to entrust our farmland as heritage and that it was being sold off to development. She saw their farms being cashed in to developers as part of their retirement plan. "In that area, I knew what people were going to say in regards to farmland preservation," said Schultz. To the aging population, the land wasn't legacy; it was retirement. Schultz also saw the impact of the lack of farmland preservation policies, noting, "Farmers have been moving from places like Courtland to Howard City into areas that do place value on farmland preservation."

Schultz always thinks about the broader system at hand, and she's concerned about the economic impact and the ability of our state to maintain a strong agricultural heritage. "A farmer should have the ability to pay his wages and still have an affordable product for market," she notes. "And access—making sure everyone in our urban neighborhoods has access to good food—that should also be of importance."

As a planner at the city level, Schultz doesn't have immediate governance over county farmland preservation issues. She does, however, have the power to endorse policy that encourages and supports community gardens and proposes land use and zoning for urban farming, markets and food-based businesses like restaurants and food trucks. She can also help support other zoning issues, including the keeping of chickens—the new mascot for the urban farmer.

Schultz's work has gained much support from longtime food advocates like Tom Cary. A Grand Rapidian and farmer, Cary has been active in the food community since the late 1990s, when he was a researcher at the West Michigan Environmental Action Council. "The thinking was, if we could make a local food economy work, then we could attach other pieces to it and make a real local economy," he notes.[5]

Cary felt that he needed to step up and make a call to action. He soon found himself engaging more at the national level of food-systems research, as well as connecting with regional leaders. "It made me passionate about the possibilities of a local food system," he says. "It made it really clear that a lot could be done." Cary knew that it would take organizing and educating people and governments, building trust between urban consumers and local farmers, local policy changes and a willingness for people to take ownership of their food system and what they ate. Cary wanted to see these people come together to set a direction for the future of the local and regional food system. The first official gathering of these early local food conversations happened in September 2011 with the all-volunteer Greater Grand Rapids Food System Council.

Questions started to be asked. Who has access to good food—only those who can afford it? Where can it be found? Are the grocery stores that sell more affordable produce located near people that struggle in poverty, or do they only have access to convenience stores? How are we going to help kids learn where their food comes from? And the growers—is starting a new farm possible for young people? What about fair wages for those people growing the food? What does it mean to try to make a fair food system for all?

Cynthia Price, Cary's colleague and co-founder of the Greater Grand Rapids Food Systems Council, recalls the early days of bringing people together to form the coalition:

> *Put very simply, people were just beginning to be interested in eating local food, but they had no idea where to get it. African Americans and economically disadvantaged people were no part of the conversation, and people were just beginning to "get" food miles, as in, "Why do we grow all those apples up on the Alpine Ridge but the ones available at the store are from Washington state?" The only people who understood that farmers realize very little profit from each consumer dollar spent were the farmers. Connections were only just beginning to be made between the lack of healthy, high-nutrition food and the prevalence of life-threatening diseases. Almost*

no one had any idea that anything at the policy level, especially the Farm Bill, influenced their lives.[6]

Over the next ten years, the volunteer council helped catalyze many local food efforts and build awareness around local food in Grand Rapids. Cary and Price helped the city review its infrastructure for community gardening. "When we first began looking into community gardens, their support structure, Lots of Growth [a now-defunct community gardening organization active in the 1990s] was just closing its doors, and we were losing gardens left and right," explained Cary. "The city had no positive policy regarding gardens—public or private. The city administration at that time basically just tolerated them." Policy from the 1970s allowed for "allotment gardens." The city was responsible for making a list of available properties within the city and providing support for these gardens. Local food advocates like Price and Cary worked with Shultz on recommendations to address policies for community gardens, chickens and markets. "I changed ordinances to be more lenient for the development of community gardens, and I also had to address some of the zoning issues for the markets because of this process, based on the white papers outlining food-policy barriers in policy for urban agriculture," explained Schultz. "What most people don't realize is that often they don't need city permission to start a community garden…as long as they don't violate building codes for structures."

CHICKEN FIGHT

While the city planner and several commissioners are internal advocates for positive food-policy change, working with the city hasn't been without its challenges for activists within the local food movement. You might not need a permit to start a community garden in Grand Rapids, but in a city recognized by the United Nations for its sustainability practices,[7] it is not legal to compost, keep urban hens or raise bees within city limits.

For several years, activists in Grand Rapids have been working diligently to get progressive food policy passed at the city level to allow a reasonable amount of urban homesteading activities such as composting and the keeping of urban hens.

In 2008, the local food movement was about to hit a groundswell, as sales of vegetable seeds, transplants and gardening supplies shot through the roof. Chickens also became a part of that search for affordable, healthy food, with healthy eggs at an affordable price. At the same time, the global economy was tanking, and citizens interested in urban agriculture began organizing. They wanted to volunteer their time and expertise to work alongside city staffers to help determine a process to allow urban hens. Then, in 2009, Grand Rapids citizens designed a task force, organizing via social media channels, to start to design favorable chicken legislation that the city could support and the people of Grand Rapids would respectfully follow.

But for the City of Grand Rapids, the timing couldn't have been worse. Municipal budgets were also taking significant hits. Layoffs were happening left and right, and staff members were overwhelmed. The commission was not interested in entertaining ordinances that would bring undue or significant burden on limited staff resources while public health and safety still had to be maintained.

In good faith, citizens on the task force helped take up the slack where the city needed help. The group dedicated volunteer time to the city, benchmarking other cities of comparable size (and political leanings), including Madison, Rochester, Ann Arbor, Brooklyn and Salt Lake City, with urban agriculture clauses and policy. The task force reached out to the municipal officials in these cities who had successfully developed a process for licensing and tracking violations and maintenance for the chickens.

Holly Bechiri, local food advocate and backyard farmer, was a member of this task force and leveraged support from fellow urban farmers in Los Angeles. Erik Knutsen, Los Angeles food advocate and author of *The Urban Homestead*, wrote the following to Holly:

> *All across the United States, people are realizing the value of access to fresh, local food. Keeping a few hens in your backyard is part of this movement. It's the kind of activity Thomas Jefferson would be proud of. Just a handful of hens will keep a family self-sufficient in eggs, important in these tough times. Here in Los Angeles, hens are legal, but roosters are not in most zoning areas. I urge you to consider welcoming these beautiful birds and the wholesome food they bring.*[8]

Other residents in favor of sustainability helped advocate the cause. Anne Guilfoyle, a longtime Grand Rapids resident, community volunteer and wellness advocate, wrote to the city, "To support this legislation is consistent with your goals of encouraging healthy lifestyles, healthy eating and sustainability. While I share the concerns that some have expressed, if we are going to truly walk the walk [of health and sustainability as a city] we need to permit this urban chicken ordinance to pass."[9]

Meanwhile, the forces wanting to derail the chicken advocates were growing in number, led by Herbruck's Poultry Ranch, a large-scale chicken hatchery and farm. Herbruck's and other organizations against residents keeping chickens established arguments ranging from avian flu concerns to cleanliness, noise and other disease.[10] Small-scale farmers found this opposition from the factory farmers both ironic and laughable. "The keeping of a few healthy hens in a backyard setting is not a factor in the spread of avian influenza, as the CDC and USDA, the highest-level sources of official information on health and agriculture in this country, have publicly stated," pointed out Stephanie Pierce, a local permaculture farmer.[11] With the ordinance on the desks of their commissioners, the citizens felt they had a win in their favor. But when the final chicken ordinance went up for vote in August 2010, it was defeated.

First Ward commissioners Dave Shaffer and Walt Gutowski Jr. joined with Third Ward commissioner Elias Lumpkins to force a tie vote that killed the ordinance. Citizens cited backroom dealings and shifty politics for the defeat. Those citizens who had lobbied so very hard to support the city's interest felt abandoned. The Beerhorsts, one of the city's first homesteading families, were heartbroken over the decision but continue today to house chickens with the support of their neighbors. What happened to the rest that had chickens? Some gave them up, but some still have their birds, banking on a "don't ask, don't tell" gentlemen's agreement between the urban farmers and the city.

More than two years later, the chicken debate continues to simmer on a low boil. Citizens continue to rally on social media, trying to design campaigns to get the chickens back on the docket. Others talk about replacing some of the commissioners with people who understand the critical role of raising and growing one's own food as part of making a livable city.

While surprised about the failed chicken vote, city planner Schultz remains hopeful. Schultz's pragmatic approach is necessary to balance the needs of growing a city's attractions—bars, restaurants, gardens, etc—with mixed-use development in neighborhoods where citizens are both living and working. "We want mixed-used neighborhoods, and we want them livable, too," she says.[12]

Farming the City

Standing in the middle of an urban lot on Wealthy Street in the streaming evening sunshine, half a dozen local men and as many young children work in the heat of the night. It is a late July summer night—one of the hottest on record—and although the sun has fallen behind the trees, the heat index is still over 90 in the middle of the city.

The garden sits on some very prominent property. Wealthy Street is home to one of Grand Rapids' main business districts and is a main thoroughfare. Cars pass along the brick-paved street while the group clears the land of cement and brush. Shovels pick away at the rock in the soil, while chainsaws clear up the brush, which is then loaded into the back of the work truck. There is hollering and laughing while the men call to each other, taking time to wipe sweaty brows and check on the smaller children lending a hand. The women also join in, performing some heavy lifting, while the rest of their families gather together to make a group meal for them to share after the work is finished. This is something they get together and do each and every Monday night.

Andy Dragt is one of the ringleaders of the group. Raised in Kalamazoo, Dragt is a longtime resident of the adjacent Baxter neighborhood of Grand Rapids, where he resides with his wife and two children. His love for his community is a central part of his family's lifestyle. And while he didn't grow up on a farm, his grandfather was one of the largest potato and onion farmers in Grant. Farming is in his blood. For Dragt, urban agriculture, gardening and cooking are all about getting the community around the same table. Dragt and five other families are tilling this urban farm in the central city of Grand Rapids as a way to reconnect with the source of their food.

Guy Bazanni, the landowner of the lot and a longtime proponent of local food and local food system infrastructure, is allowing the Uptown Farm to garden at the site for a small leasing fee. Dragt is grateful for Bazzani's continued support of local food ventures. "All I said was, 'Hey, Guy—we'd like to plant here. Maybe we could lease it for a small amount of money?' and he was like 'Yeah, just tell me what you want.' It was that easy," Dragt explains. "And as for the city, Suzanne Schultz was very helpful in making sure this was as easy as possible for us to get going on the site clearance," explains Dragt.[13]

Around the corner from Uptown Farm is Dragt's home in the Baxter community. His front-yard vegetable garden is an odd contrast to the neighboring yards. Dragt's children play in the garden out front and along the sidewalks. The girls proudly show off their vegetable gardens, the beds arranged in neat rows in front of the house. "We grow as much as we can for our family, and the kids love to come out and harvest," explains Dragt. "They will eat bok choy if they've grown it. As long as they participate in it, then they like it that much more."

Dragt sees the potential for gardens everywhere. Across from Dragt's home is a lot owned by the city, one of the few places where kids can enjoy outdoor play. "When I first moved in, I thought for sure that lot should be a garden. But all the neighborhood kids like to play in there, and it's a safe place for them to kick a ball around." Dragt pauses for a moment and then continues, "I think that's as important as a garden. I don't want to take that away from them."

In planning the Uptown Farm, Dragt and his friends researched small-scale intensive urban farming operations that were low in overhead and had the potential for positive revenue generation. "Land is a premium here," admits Dragt. "We plan to grow what we can intensively, in quick relays—three rotations of crops per season, plus winter crops. We want this to prove that you can generate a moderate return. These will be all-intensive, high-turnover vegetables—greens, herbs, parsleys, cilantros—with high market value." He continues, "The idea to begin the Uptown Farm started mostly because we just like doing it. We have people who are interested in doing it, and with a lot this size with six to eight families…it's no big deal. It's something we can do without a ton of money or anything substantial at risk. It's a low-risk perspective." Dragt's rule for the project is, "Keep your overhead low, and just do it."

Eight weeks later, the group's work has paid off. The lot, once filled with stumps, concrete and weeds, has grown into a fully functional urban market farm. Restaurants like Grove and Bartertown and retail organic food suppliers like Doorganics have begun selling the greens and herbs for their hyperlocal specials. Uptown Farm is truly tilling and trailblazing the way to new markets for their crops.

As the leaves begin to change color in the fall, the Dragts turn their attention to gathering friends and family for a harvest celebration. Dragt recounts the growing season's challenges: "Water will always be a challenge on vacant land. Also, learning how much and how fast crops will come in was a challenge…we planted way too much arugula and couldn't move it all at once when it was ready to be harvested."[14] The Uptown Farm also had success with hardy crops like kale and red choy.

Dragt is excited to continue to connect with others around the city interested in trying this method of farming. He has a vision of urban farmers learning together at Uptown Farm, growing food for their families and for their own income. He sees a cooperative team running the farm. "Imagine someone in our neighborhood that comes here and gets inspired," says Dragt. "We'd like this to begin to be a cooperative of growers—this can be a way to help create talent in the community."

Diversity in the Garden

While there might be an open invite to join Dragt at his proverbial dinner table, not everyone feels the culture of community in Grand Rapids that Dragt has helped to cultivate at the Uptown Farm.

Grand Rapids is quite diverse and has a rich history of immigration and immigrants establishing neighborhoods throughout our community. From the Italian neighborhoods south on Division to the Polish Westside and today's Hispanic corridor along Grandville and the strong Asian community south of the Central City, Grand Rapids' vibrant diversity is something that needs to be invested in and celebrated.

One struggle that must be addressed by the local food advocates is the fact that there are many people living in Grand

Seeds Are Common Property. Print by Alynn Guerra.

Rapids outside the dominant white, Christian culture who are not able to participate fully in the "local food scene" because of a variety of social and economic barriers. Lisa Oliver-King, food sovereignty advocate of Our

29

Kitchen Table, shoots it straight when others may not feel as comfortable discussing the underlying race and immigration issues. "The reality is that Grand Rapids is a highly segregated city, and this is important to point out, because it is primarily the white, economically well-off sectors of this city that have been benefiting from the 'local' food efforts."[15]

Bing Goei, Grand Rapids business leader and advocate for minority business owners, is known for his tenacity and belief in the power of the people from different cultures. Goei notes:

> *Here on the southwest side, we have so many cultures from Latin America. We have a large Cuban population in the neighborhood…one bakery owner recently told me that he needs to order a specialty Cuban bread straight from Cuba. I learned that if he had access to ovens, he would be able to have this special bread made here in town. We need to focus on building up these businesses.*[16]

For Goei, diversity is a core value in everything that he does in the community, and as a civic leader, it is the central tenet of his leadership platform. Born of Chinese parents in Indonesia, Goei arrived to the United States with his family via the Netherlands in the 1960s. Entrepreneurial at a young age, Goei started his own flower business in high school. Thanks to his passion and perseverance, Goei's Eastern Floral business generates over $5 million in annual revenue and employs sixty year-round staff in over seven locations.[17]

In addition to supporting the growth of woman-owned and minority businesses, Goei has also been a champion for urban agriculture.

> *I have had a vision for growing greenhouses atop the Blodgett landfill on the southwest side. I have been trying to get the city to consider adding greenhouses to allow for food and flower production. It's not build-able land, so we should use it for something with purpose. Imagine rows of greenhouses on the empty landfill…imagine the jobs that could be created and what that could mean for the people living in the neighborhoods in the area.*

Goei is active in the community with projects such as the Bethany Christian Services, a local nonprofit that supports the relocation of refugees by managing the immigration process and helping establish residency. Serving refugees from countries such as Bhutan, Burma, Eritrea, Iraq, the Congo and South Sudan, Bethany secures green cards for the immigrants and helps them find job opportunities. Part of that relocation process includes helping refugees obtain access to land to cultivate their own subsistence gardens, in which the new immigrants can plant the foods of their homeland for their families. These programs are crucial in helping provide the newly relocated families with resources for good, healthful and local food.

Bethany has been operating three sizable community gardens over the past three years in Grand Rapids and Kentwood, with over sixty families growing food in subsistence gardens in fifteen-by-thirty-foot plots, and staff members say that there is now a waiting list with other families.[18] The Bethany staff sees the growing interest on behalf of the gardeners to gain access to their own land to become farmers—and possibly agricultural business owners. This would be an opportunity for them to truly participate in the local food economy as new immigrants and set them on their way with ensured food security.

Goei is supportive of the creativity in Bethany's garden outreach and the potential in a refugee farmer-training program here in the city. "This kind of thinking is what we need," he says. "A program like this could give tremendous power to the immigrants living here. This can give the refugees an opportunity for the new life in America they dream of."

Goei's focus is not solely on the food. He wants his advocacy work to result in a Grand Rapids that embraces, recognizes and celebrates the positive power of the variety of cultures living in the city. "Grand Rapids should be helping to highlight these vibrant cultural communities in our area, and we should be helping new immigrant groups and cultures thrive with economic development opportunities available through urban gardening and farming." Bing sees this as a win for everyone. "By focusing on Grand Rapids' international flavor and highlighting that we are more diverse," he says, "we will create demand for these small business owners. And that will enrich our communities all over the city."

Chapter 3

Feeding the Movement: Farms and Tables

When tillage begins, other arts follow. The farmers, therefore, are the founders of human civilization.
—Daniel Webster

Farmers are at the heart of the local food movement. They are the connection between the sun, water and the soil. Their hands cultivate and harvest the vegetables and tend to the animals. While new urban farmers like Dragt till the way for new urban gardens and farms, it was the dedication of a core group of farmers that have helped root the growing local food movement in the Greater Grand Rapids area.

Grand Rapids remains within close proximity to fertile land, and the area has rich history in both food production and production of flowers and landscaping dating back well over one hundred years. Today, nearly 31 percent of acreage in Kent County is devoted to agricultural production, with crops ranging in variety from dairy, poultry and vegetables to orchards, grains and corn.[19]

ON THE FARM

Karen Lubbers of Lubbers Family Farm is a local matriarch for the local food movement. Since the late 1990s, their farm has served as an anchor for foodies and activists alike, helping to address the issues of access and education while balancing them with the vital economics of being a small-scale, organic food producer and maintaining a commitment to being good stewards over their land. "Economics are driven by the resources you have available to you and what you're passionate about,"[20] explains Lubbers. "In our case, we have a limited number of tillable acres relatively close to an urban center. Land here is very expensive, so expanding our acreage is not an option."

From the raw milk Community Supported Agriculture (CSA) program to the on-site farmers' market, creamery and bakery, Lubbers explains that the

In addition to being land stewards and food producers, the Lubbers farmers are educators. "We think of our farm as a three-legged stool," says Lubbers. "The third leg is education and outreach. We do this through events and speaking engagements—it is extremely helpful in telling our story." *Photo courtesy of Karen Lubbers.*

farm needs to stay in ecological balance with the limited resources the land offers it. To stay competitive, Lubbers Family Farm produces only a limited quantity of high-value items, as opposed to a larger quantity of low-value items. "We focus on quality," Lubbers explains.

In addition to being land stewards and food producers, the Lubbers farmers are educators. "We think of our farm as a three-legged stool," says Lubbers. "The third leg is education and outreach. We do this through events and speaking engagements—it is extremely helpful in telling our story."

Farmers are doing more than just growing food for the community. They are stewards of the land and know most intimately the need to take care of the lands and waters that sustain us. The impacts of conventional, chemical-based agriculture and factory farms can be environmentally devastating—particularly in an area as ecologically sensitive as the Great Lakes. Farmers like Lubbers are helping our community make the connection between healthy land and water and the food we eat. At the top of these environmental concerns—both locally and globally—is water scarcity. As seasonal weather patterns become less predictable, farmers will need to adapt their farming strategies and work with the land to be able to endure these ever-changing patterns. As part of the Great Lakes Watershed, home to the second-largest body of fresh water in the world, water conservation and preservation is becoming increasingly important, particularly in light of the ever-growing global water crisis.

Local environmental advocates support sustainability-minded farmers like Lubbers who are choosing practices that work with nature's systems rather than against it. Rachel Hood, director of the West Michigan Environmental Action Council, states that our most pressing environmental issues here in West Michigan are the loss of farmland, sustainable farming practices, soil preservation and water scarcity. Hood is concerned about the impact of the farming practices by large-scale agriculture in West Michigan. "West Michigan and Michigan as a whole are agricultural powerhouses. Farming practices have a huge impact on water quality,"[21] explains Hood. "Michigan is full of concentrated animal feeding operations (CAFOs), which are known polluters, contributing animal waste to our water system and creating E-coli breakouts. We are polluting our precious fresh water. If we don't farm sustainably, we won't sustain our water quality."

When it comes to food and local agriculture, the end goal of environmental protection will result in the actual preservation of our agricultural heritage. "If we want to sustain our farming heritage, and if we want to protect our water for generations, then we had better support farmers with good practices," says Hood. "Michigan's agricultural practices need to be linked to soil conservation and water protection if we are to continue being a major contributor to the U.S. food basket."

Michael VanderBrug, organic farmer and owner of Trillium Haven Farm, shares these concerns and ponders what the future of agriculture will look like. VanderBrug, having been an organic farmer on his land for over ten years, is well aware of the complexity of this issue and the difficulties large and small-scale farms are currently having in regards to climate change and agriculture economics in a global agriculture industry.

As certified organic farmers, VanderBrug and his wife, Anja Mast, have experimented with different business strategies to continue to feed their local community with good, healthy food grown in the rich soil of their sixty-acre farm in Jenison. They have experience in running a five-hundred-family Community Supported Agriculture (CSA) program and most recently expanded their operations to include a farm-owned restaurant in the city of Grand Rapids called Trillium Haven as means to help supply their farm with more steady income. But these pioneer endeavors haven't been without risk.[22]

Farmer Tom Cary credits Michael and Anja's courage, persistence and perseverance in staying the course over the past ten years, noting that Trillium Haven Farm has been "raising the bar for local food and the possibilities of Community Supported Agriculture and showing that anyone can start farming and succeed." For Cary himself, it was a revelation to step into farming:

> *Despite growing up in a suburb and lacking the experience, never having thought of farming as a job or career, I'm now working alongside others growing good food that people enjoy—and I can support myself doing it. It is still surprising that farming can be so accessible as a career. I saw it happen at Lubbers Farm and with Michael and Anja, but becoming it was different.*[23]

Trillium Haven Farm has influenced many others in the Grand Rapids area to pursue farming. Just south of the city, on a sixty-acre farm with a few outbuildings and a home, young Ben Bylsma takes a moment to observe the growth of the tomatoes in his greenhouse.

Bylsma's educational background isn't in agriculture; he was a liberal arts student. A Spanish major, Bylsma studied international development and was originally a math student. Bylsma is learning by doing, and his start in farming has its roots in his experiences as an intern at Trillium Haven Farm.

With his baby in hand, this new farmer walks down aisles of cucumbers, checking on the plants. It is late August, and Bylsma laughs about getting things under control. "Everything needs to be pruned and trimmed," he says. "It's a tomato jungle in here."[24] Bylsma has been getting his coaching from growers in Ontario, Canada, home to one of the largest production centers for greenhouse tomatoes.

For a small grower like Bylsma, the wholesale greenhouse tomato market is hard to compete with. He notes:

This spring, the wholesale market was offering their tomatoes from Florida and Canada at $0.20 to $0.30 on the pound. Restaurants weren't going to pay my $1.50 per pound that I needed to make to cover my costs. I can't compete with that. So it forced me to really find my niche at the farmers' market. People were really excited to get early season tomatoes. We

Farmer Ben Bylsma as an intern at Trillium Haven Farm. *Photo by Shane Folkertsma.*

were selling at the markets to consumers and to other vendors for other markets…I was moving about 1,500 pounds of tomatoes a week.

Despite the growing popularity of local food, it is still difficult for small-scale farmers to make a decent living—it requires good budgeting and creative planning. Bylsma values a diversified income for his farm, calculating inputs and outputs all the time to make sure what he is doing is financially viable. He and his wife bought their farm in 2010 with a business loan. "These economic times make it really hard to get financing," he says. "When I look at how much I need to make a square foot, I need to make five times what I am currently making."

Pastured heirloom chickens run around as Bylsma gets to his morning chores. The chickens are being raised for Trillium Haven's restaurant. "I bring the birds to Zeeland for slaughter because of the licensed facility," Bylsma says. "It's not a moneymaker. I don't make money back on the labor, but I do get ten chickens for my family for keeping the coops, and that gets us through the winter."

But Bylsma doesn't just focus on the bottom line. He realizes his role as a land steward, and there is tension between what he can do to keep his farm afloat and his vision. The diversity in the wild spaces is abundant, as the ditches and hedgerows and borders of the greenhouses are alive with native plants. On one edge of the field, Bylsma is leasing out the land to a corn grower. Motioning to the crop of corn, he says, "I think what I will do is plant a rotation of crops that I can use for fuel so that I can get away from natural gas in the greenhouses. Right now, I just don't have the money to convert it all over to bio-fuel, and natural gas is really cheap right now, so there isn't an urgency. I can only do so much all at once."

Tom Cary encourages all new farmers to plan and learn carefully:

Start with rented land (which is very affordable) with money saved up and stick to the basics. Do what you can afford, and make a really good budget. On the income side, be as conservative as you can. Don't expect to make a profit in the first couple of years, especially if you are going to be sinking money into equipment, infrastructure, etc. Get as much experience as you can working for conventional and/or organic farmers, because they have techniques and knowledge that is really beneficial. And DO NOT (unless there is just no way or you don't have enough patience) start in debt!

For VanderBrug, it is encouraging to see new farmers take risks and go off on their own. He believes that the growing movement needs to be rooted in continued community support. With that, VanderBrug is hopeful for the future. "West Michigan has made some strong moves in the right direction, and the support for local and sustainable agriculture has never been more apparent," he notes. "There are numerous small and artisanal farms that have been created in the past ten years, and it has been exciting to watch. Still, we have a long way to go."

AT THE TABLES

Over the past ten years, the Grand Rapids restaurant scene has slowly added establishments that feature local, farm-fresh produce. It hasn't been an easy course. From procurement to preparation, choosing to support local producers is a significant amount of work on the end of the restaurant. It requires a shift in menu design and ordering and even demands a higher caliber of talent in the kitchen, requiring staff that know how to prepare whole foods from scratch into meals that diners will appreciate.

Having been on the supplier end of the developing farm-to-table scene, providing vegetables for restaurants that included the J.W. Marriott's six. one.six and Marie Catrib's, farmers Michael VanderBrug and Anja Mast of Trillium Haven decided to get into the restaurant business themselves—with the farmer actually owning the table. Located in the bustling neighborhood of Eastown, this husband-and-wife team now has a popular restaurant with a curated menu that is seasonal and reflective of their land's bounty.

This new innovation on the farm-to-table restaurant concept would not have been possible twenty or even ten years ago in Grand Rapids. One of the first restaurants in Grand Rapids credited for pushing the local palate and promoting local foods is downtown's own San Chez. Since 1992, San Chez has been serving up small plates Spanish tapas-style, along with Chilean wines, Spanish paella, harissa sauce and garlic, garlic, garlic. Former chef Casey Bell took inspiration from his time living in Spain in crafting early menus for San Chez, admitting, "It wasn't easy because I couldn't get the same ingredients."[25] Bell recalls trying to re-create a classic Spanish paella for Grand Rapids eaters. "We wanted paella, a staple dish in Spain, to be our signature entree right from the beginning," he says. "To make it as authentically as we could, I used a short-grain rice that was closest to the traditional bomba rice in Spain. But in the '90s, diners were used to long-grain rice and thought they were eating mush! By educating diners—which our staff has always been great at doing—we were able to keep the dish on the menu."

San Chez was an early adopter and promoter of local producers and artisan foods. Sobie Meats and Dancing Goat Creamery were two of the first vendors San Chez used for its menu. Additionally, the restaurant hosted local food meet-ups to help grow the local food movement. Celebrating twenty years and counting, San Chez continues to refine its menu to fit the ever-evolving tastes of its diners.

In addition to Dan Gelder's San Chez, Greg Gilmore became another early pioneer of the downtown restaurant scene with his purchase and salvation of the dilapidated Judson's Grocery Warehouse at the corner of Monroe and Fulton—now known as the popular "Big Old Building" (the B.O.B.). Today, the B.O.B. is a local destination for visitors and residents alike to the downtown area. But when the building was renovated back in the late '90s, it was one of the few restaurants that pushed the culinary limits of the Grand Rapids' meat-and-potatoes palate. Gilmore recalls the difficulty in trying to sell his patrons on worldly cuisine. "In the early days, people didn't understand the food—it was too exotic, too spicy, this and that," says Gilmore.[26] "Local culinary talent Angus Campbell put the menu together. It was really awesome, but people just didn't understand it." Gilmore accepted that reality of culinary defeat. "We had to adapt our menus a fair amount and become mainstream," he says. But Gilmore is hopeful about his patrons' palates, noting, "Today, Grand Rapids is definitely less meat-and-potatoes. When we put something new and unique on one of our menus, it is better received. And now, the focus is on local and fresh." Planned along with the slotted expansion of the B.O.B.'s facility is the addition of an outdoor, four-season biergarten that will showcase not only the local Grand Rapids brews but also the quality of Michigan beer from brewers of the Michigan Brewers Guild.

Gilmore takes pride in the fact that the Gilmore Collection has been sourcing local for its restaurants since 1978 with their first restaurant, the Thornapple. With the size of the Gilmore Collection today, this is not an easy task. "We buy approximately $8 million of food a year for all of our restaurants—we want to buy local. We need to gain any advantage we can, and of course we want to support our local agricultural economy. But recognizing the volume that we need to do…it is hard to find a supplier that, for example, can get us a whole chicken breast for the entire collection for an entire season."

Buying local for multiple restaurants takes a strong network of local producers, a strong kitchen team and time. No one knows this better than Executive Chef Patrick Wise of the Essence Restaurant Group. Wise, now executive chef at Grove, has been cultivating relationships with farmers and the restaurants for Essence since he was twenty-three years old and working downtown at Bistro Bella Vita. "We grew these relationships over time," he says. "S&S Lamb is now raising duck, chicken, lamb and pheasants for our restaurants—all up from just ordering three items. It was a slow process—over five or six years. Now it is a relationship that is there for the long haul, and it works for everybody."[27] Wise reflects on the difficulty of growing an intentional, local procurement system, noting, "When we first started with Nathan Creswick and his farm, we were in over our heads and ended up over-committed. Now it is great. We have a totally different approach to working together." For Wise, sourcing is key. "I am not going to put anything on our menu that I don't know its source," he says. "You can trust me to know what's being put on your plate. This is all built on trust. I even help with seed selection with the farmers and make the commitment to sourcing the vegetables from particular farms so that I know the food's source."

Wise is aware that there are limitations to what restaurants can do to source locally, especially when working on a larger scale. Wise focuses on "head-to-tail" cooking as a means to maximize the variety. Foods come into the restaurant in their raw form and need to be prepped and prepared. Much of the restaurant's food is made from scratch. "Procuring local for a large-scale operation—It's not going to happen overnight," says Wise. "It's a different way of ordering and maintaining inventory and creating menus. It's not like calling Sysco."

The Essence staff planted a garden plot in the Hillcrest Community Garden to be a source of produce and to help the kitchen and front-of-house staff make that visceral connection to the season in which the food is grown. Wise also requires his staff to do extra professional development and "book reports" on different aspects of their growers and local agriculture. This helps them to connect people with local suppliers and farmers like Kingma's, the Fulton Street Market or Sobie's. "We like to tell our guests where they can go out and get these products," says Wise. "And these reports help develop my staff as experts."

Wise considers these extra steps a testament to Essence's focus on quality. Social responsibility is also at the top of Essence's value set. Wise and his staff venture out to the farms with local school kids and then back into the kitchen with their parents, showing them the full farm-to-table experience. "Last summer, we took a group of six- to ten-year-olds out to Charlie Ham's farm and then to the farmers' market with their parents. We gave them tokens to do some of their own shopping. They were eating raw radishes—all city kids, some of whom would have never gotten a chance to get out onto a farm like that." For Wise and the Essence Group, community engagement like that makes a difference. "If kids don't get hooked or parents don't get hooked, we won't change anything," he says.

The employee-owned and operated Bartertown Diner is another Grand Rapids restaurant looking to make a lasting change in the community. The brainchild of entrepreneur Ryan Cappelletti, a local restaurateur whose own roots were founded in helping establish the popular Brick Road Pizza, Bartertown has grown up from grass roots. The diner embraces the belief, which is contrary to most of the industry, that it's possible to create a restaurant environment that is good for the eater, the worker and the food. Here, everyone from the dishwasher to the host earns the same wage and a share of the tips, reflecting the work that each person puts in on a particular day. Matt Russell, vegan baker for Bartertown, boils down their restaurant's philosophy: "Equal pay and equal say."[28]

Bartertown's cooperative business model is unique to the restaurant industry, which is infamous for its unfair and inequitable labor standards. To Russell, the equal ownership structure at Bartertown is significant. He states:

Out of chef whites and onto the farm. Grove's executive chef Patrick Wise visiting the local farms that supply the Essence Group. *Photo courtesy of The Image Shoppe.*

Most everyone [at Bartertown] *has come from a situation where they felt like they were treated unfairly, whether because of a boss or a structure of hierarchy between different jobs. We wanted to create a place where there is no boss. The workers are the bosses, and they decide each week how the restaurant is run. They should be the ones benefiting from their work, not some suit who stops in every so often to tell everyone they need to work more and get paid less because times are tough.*

Along with an egalitarian structure, the menu is vegan and nearly all local. The fruits and vegetables are all from local farms not more than twenty miles away. "Our breads are made in town with organic flours," says Russell. "Our oils, nuts, spices and other items that aren't necessarily made in Michigan are still organic and sourced, whenever possible, from companies that are employee-owned. And Michigan really has some great farmers."

Russell notes that the Bartertown staff regularly visits the farms to learn more about where the food comes from and how it is grown. "Ham Family Farms in Allendale provides the majority of our fruits and vegetables," he says. "Charlie Ham is a lot of fun to work with. We get a lot of our bread from Ken Freestone of I Love Bread and Butter and our raw desserts from Jeremy Kuhn of Deliciosity. Our coffee comes from Direct Trade Coffee Company. We are pretty close with all our suppliers."

Bartertown's menu is a testament to the notion that eating healthy, plant-based meals year-round can also be based on foods procured from Michigan. "The main constraint we find when it comes to locally grown produce is making the most of different harvesting seasons," explains Russell. "Tomatoes and sweet corn are incredibly abundant, but it seems like they're just coming in one day and then the season is over the following week."

Unlike the Gilmore Collection or Essence Restaurant Group, Bartertown's size allows it to be nimble and flexible in both its purchasing and its quick menu adaptations. "We've found several different ways to make a pesto that doesn't rely on basil," notes Russell. "There have been pizza sauces made from sweet potatoes and squash, and we've even done barbecue and hot sauces without tomatoes."

The kicker? Bartertown is also one of the most affordable local establishments in Grand Rapids. Making food that workers can afford is one of the biggest values the restaurant has. And it's vegan. For Russell, veganism is a personal way of life: "I think food should provide honest nutrition and sustenance first, then flavor and innovation."

Bartertown isn't the first Grand Rapids restaurant to bring vegetarian fare to Grand Rapids. Gaia Café's menu hasn't changed a bit in over a decade, still famous for its Mean Green Burrito and Miso Soup. Gaia had the vegetarian market all but cornered through the early 2000s until Marie Catrib launched her own Mediterranean delicatessen in the midst of the East Hills Center of the Universe Building in 2005. Upon the deli's opening, Catrib and her son Fouad created nearly an overnight cult following, with regular lunch lines stretching out the door starting at 11:30 a.m. Relying largely on local ingredients, nearly everything at Marie's is made from scratch, including an expanding menu of gluten-free and vegan items.

While the demand for more plant-based cuisine continues to grow, Russell resigns that not everyone that comes into the restaurant gets it. "There are always some people who come in, see the menu and then leave," he says, "but there are just as many—if not more—who decide to stay and try something new, and I bet about 90 percent of them come back." He notes that it's a delicate balance between quality ingredients and simple, accessible cooking:

I don't think anyone objects to a vegan menu that specializes in local ingredients. There are some regulars that have told me they almost always eat meat for dinner but that because we support local farms they are willing to come in and eat our food, too. Some people find ways to complain about anything—they'll say that a vegan and/or locally sourced restaurant is pretentious or cliquish, but then they come in and try some two-dollar tacos with local greens and chickpeas, and their opinion is changed.

Over the past several years, Russell has seen the demand for vegan and gluten-free baking increase in Grand Rapids enough that he is on his way to launching his own vegan baked goods establishment. Russell's baking endeavors began while in college. "I couldn't afford much, and it forced me to be creative with things like frozen peas and rice and beans," he admits. "After a while, I just got into vegan baking and cooking from there."

In addition to being the vegan baker at Bartertown, Russell runs Wednesday Evening Cookies, a vegan cookie subscription service. As an avid cyclist, Russell delivers his vegan baked goods to his clients by bicycle around the city. "It's not incredibly hard delivering by bike if the weather is nice," he says. "I recently got a trailer that I can haul about nine ten-by-ten boxes in, and each of those holds about two dozen cookies or one dozen cupcakes. If it's anything four boxes or less, I strap them all together and just hold them with my right hand while I ride." Bicycle delivery is a signature of Russell's business, but to him, it is more than that. "I think I like delivering by bicycle because I am really proud of the desserts I bake. I want to put just a little more effort into getting them to people. You ride a few miles up some big hills, and you're just that much more excited to drop off a dozen cupcakes."

This sense of pride is seen through and through in the work of those in our food community. George Aquino, Grand Rapids food writer and general manager of the J.W. Marriott Grand Rapids, thinks highly of Grand Rapids' growing restaurant scene. Having moved to the area in 1996, Aquino remembers the early days when there were limited dining options for residents and visitors alike. "I am very proud to say that our city is now one of the best foodie towns of its size in the United States," he notes. "Downtown is attracting more residents, and this will eventually lead to more diverse restaurant options for the locals."[29]

Aquino, born in Manila and a world traveler, has an adventurous and global palate. But don't expect only highbrow tastes from this foodie. Frequently, his reviews will feature his favorite pho restaurant or one of his favorite places for *tacos de lengua*. Aquino knows comfort food and frequents the neighborhood bar as much as the popular farm-to-table scene. "The local food scene has come a long way," he notes. "And there is still more room to grow."

Chapter 4

Tilling and Trailblazing: Future Food Artisans

Food should make you feel good, and "feeling good" doesn't just indicate the richness or flavor. It should make you feel happy that you made it. It should make you feel honorable about the ingredients you used. It should make you feel contented when you're eating it alone and feel taken care of when you're served it. It can make you think, make you remember, make you wonder and make you discover.
—Tory O'Haire, The Starving Artist

With the increase in popularity of local artisan foods, there's never been a better time for the entrepreneur to take his idea to market. Whether it's a vegan bakery, coffee shop or underground supper club, there is an opportunity to succeed in the niche food business.

THE CULINARY UNDERGROUND

Tory O'Haire, aka The Starving Artist, knows craftsmanship. Private chef, cocktail artist, herbologist and underground supper-club owner, O'Haire is filled with passion for food and the ever-growing food culture in Grand Rapids. A native Grand Rapidian, O'Haire at one time yearned to move elsewhere to pursue his culinary adventures. But like many other young professionals, O'Haire has decided to remain in Grand Rapids to be a part of growing the local food scene.

A seasoned restaurant-industry professional, Tory has had experience in all aspects of the business, preparing him for the current culinary freedom that he cultivates as his own free agent, The Starving Artist. "I've worked in Grand Rapids' restaurants and bars for over ten years, having done everything from busboy to bartender to manager to executive chef," he notes. "I finally realized that I didn't want to be in that industry anymore until I had my own place. So I stepped back and started The Starving Artist."[30]

O'Haire needed a break from the industry but kept the cooking and creative juices flowing:

> *Food is my passion, and I couldn't imagine having nothing to do with it, but I was so burnt out on the restaurant industry. This was just before it started to pick up in Grand Rapids. I needed a break. I thought, "Well, I bet if I quit all my jobs and started asking people if I could cook for them, I'll either figure out a way to make it work or get the power shut*

Tory O'Haire, The "Starving Artist." *Photo by Michelle Smith.*

off." Low and behold, three years of hard work later, I still have the lights on.

One of O'Haire's most successful culinary creations is the area's first underground supper club, the Full Moon Supper Club. Having always had a knack for manifesting wild ideas into being, O'Haire talks about the inception of the concept:

One Sunday, after I had some friends over for a really exceptional dinner, I asked myself, "Why don't we do dinner parties every month?" I dwelled on that thought for about thirty minutes before I decided that there was absolutely no reason not to do parties monthly! It began as a group of predominantly my social circle, but then everyone started bringing friends, and then their friends started bringing friends, and before long, we had almost half of the table populated by new faces to everyone.

Now in its third year, the Full Moon Supper Club has over five hundred active followers. O'Haire is proud that people looking for a creative, off-the-wall culinary experience seek him out. "People offer to host us at their homes and businesses all the time," he says. "It's an inexpensive social experience to learn about new food and enjoy a community fellowship. It's like networking without all the awful parts. With wine."

O'Haire doesn't mince words when it comes to some of the challenges of growing the diner's expectations around quality and cost. "The two biggest issues with the industry in a city like this are the economic culture that the area has built and the fear of the unknown or unusual," he notes. O'Haire struggles with what he describes as an "addiction to 'bargain' corporate restaurants," claiming that the diners do not understand how much things actually cost and thus don't place a fair value on the food. He also believes that it is tough for professional chefs to make it in the Grand Rapids culinary market:

Every chef in this city knows that for every legitimately creative dish you put on the menu, you must also put a chicken-and-potatoes dish on there. People just don't want to try things they're not used to in this city. I remember at one restaurant, I had to practically pay people to eat the duck, which was easily the best dish on the menu. It's just duck—it's barely weirder than chicken!

But these challenges aren't enough to keep O'Haire away or jumping ship to a different market like San Francisco or Chicago that has a more established food culture. He's got his money and time betting on Grand Rapids. "I've got a few projects up my sleeve that I'm putting into motion," he says with a smile. "You'll see my first brick-and-mortar food business open within the year, and you might even see my restaurant shortly thereafter! I really love being one of the 'movers and shakers' in this young culinary community that Grand Rapids is developing, and I plan to take full participation in it."

INTO THE KITCHEN

Part of growing a good food economy is ensuring that the physical infrastructure is in place so that budding food entrepreneurs have a space to create and prototype their food products as they grow their business and take their ideas to market. Costs of capital outlay for a new food business can be limiting, and having access to affordable, licensed kitchen space to develop their projects can significantly boost the likelihood that newly launched food business will succeed.

Across the country, states are passing Cottage Food legislation to allow food artisans to produce jams, jellies, breads, pies and other food sundries in unlicensed kitchens to be sold at farmers' markets and farm stands. There are some limitations, however, and these products cannot be sold in retail establishments like grocery stores or specialty retailers.

Uptown Kitchen, the brainchild of Kelly LeCoy, opened its doors in February 2012 as a means to create a space for food entrepreneurs to launch a product and take it to the retail market with low overhead. Located in the heart of the Eastown neighborhood, Uptown Kitchen is home to all sorts of product development, including raw desserts, salsas, pies and sauces made by people with great ideas and a whole range of experience. "It was never a single decision at any one point…rather a snowball of events that led me to what I am doing now," laughs LeCoy.[31] While working on a class project at Calvin College in Grand Rapids, LeCoy started thinking about the impact of her food choices and what she was eating. She began to ask herself, "What's on my plate? Where is it coming from? What am I putting into my body? How is that affecting everything else in my life?"

LeCoy began researching the food system and the food industry. After attending college, LeCoy moved to Chicago, where she began working for the

Business Alliance in Rogers Park. "They had a lot of small food businesses in the neighborhood," notes LeCoy, "and I got to work with what is similar to our Local First in Grand Rapids." She began working on a business plan for an incubator kitchen to help grow more food businesses. LeCoy, who desired to return to Grand Rapids, nearly took a job at Bolthouse Farms but returned to Grand Rapids and began looking for locations for the commercial kitchen and talking to local business owners and potential food business owners.

Influential in helping LeCoy take her vision to market was Amy Ruis. Ruis, owner of Art of the Table on Wealthy Street in the Uptown neighborhood, was one of the pioneering shop owners who helped catalyze the redevelopment of the Wealthy corridor in the early 2000s. Art of the Table, which opened in October 2003, has shelves filled with epicurean goods of both international and local origin. Ruis stocks some the city's favorite local artisan suppliers, including food products from Dancing Goat Creamery, Art's Hot Salsa, Daily De-Lish Granola, Mrs. Dogs Mustard (she was a pioneer), Two Lads Winery, Blueberry Haven, Mrs. Morrison's Pepper Jelly, Founders and Patricia's Chocolate.[32] Art's Hot Salsa is one of LeCoy's clients. "Food artisans frequently come into Amy's store wanting to sell their homemade products in her retail shop, but they can't do that," explains LeCoy. "All across the country are niche incubators serving the local neighborhoods in large cities. I kept honing a business plan that could help serve Grand Rapids' needs." Uptown Kitchen helps fill the gap for local food artisans who have a niche product and want to test it in the retail marketplace without having to invest in the commercial kitchen capital infrastructure.

The demographics of Uptown Kitchen's clients are fairly diverse in terms of age, ethnicity and gender. There are hobby businesses—cookies and baked goods being sold at the farmers' market—as well as anchored businesses that LeCoy relies on as regular tenants. With one year of operations under her belt, LeCoy recognizes that her business is operating more like a commercial kitchen rather than an incubator. She notes:

I have considered offering programming on how to open a small food business. In the kitchen-incubator industry, I've looked to models like La Cusina in San Francisco, for example. Their program is incredible—they have a large staff and interns, and they accept incubators based on applications, primarily women from underserved communities. They help with all aspects of the business planning in order to help them grow over three to five years to become a brick-and-mortar establishment.

LeCoy contributes her early successes to Grand Rapids' supportive small-business environment. Her idea even secured early funding from a local business competition, 5x5, which was funded and operated by local businessman Rick DeVos. "5x5 perhaps was the first way I got the idea into the community," notes LeCoy. "Granted, it was a select part of the community, but I got a lot of good feedback." She believes that Grand Rapids' networking culture helped in the formative stages of the startup:

> *If I had maybe been in a Chicago neighborhood for a long time, and really formed a network and community to help support it, it might have worked there. But because of the sort of community that Grand Rapids is, I was able to get the word out here really quickly. And that only multiplied as other people got the word out. I haven't done much marketing; my clients have come largely by word of mouth.*

Nicholas Mika, another Grand Rapids food entrepreneur, agrees with LeCoy, attributing his own choice to stay in Grand Rapids to the ease in which a young professional entrepreneur can launch a business. Just around the corner from LeCoy's Uptown Kitchen, Nicholas Mika sits on top of his Honda and looks over his shoulder to the lot on the corner of Atlas and Wealthy Street in Eastown, where the carwash currently exists. This twenty-four-year-old Grand Rapids native might have wanderlust, but he wants to create what he finds alluring in other cities and countries. "China, Mexico, Colombia…I love traveling. It's about having a connection with a place, having a experience," continues Mika.[33] "That's why I travel overseas. I am trying to create a place where people can have similar experiences."

Mika, who also owns a locavore-type coffee establishment at the lakeshore in Muskegon, wants to build a food-artisan destination in Eastown made of shipping containers. He hopes to create a place that brings together a diverse crowd of people from the surrounding neighborhoods to enjoy foods made by local food artisans.

Mika shifts his feet and kicks at the Wealthy Street pavers on the road. He points to the plans spread out across the car in the lot. "I stay because I want to build—to create—what is missing here in Grand Rapids. Something real that will give people a sense of place."

Successful as Pie

Eastown has become a hub for food entrepreneurs, and the Uptown Kitchen is doing its part to grow food artisans with the commercial kitchen facility. One food artisan success story is that of seventeen-year-old Aliyah French, owner-baker for "Rochelle's A Little Something Sweet." Aliyah first began baking when she was thirteen, and pastry talents are in her blood. "Like the pastry work of her great-great-grandmother, Aliyah loves the details—lattices, taking care of the edges," says her mother, Lysandra French. "Even the crumbles she likes neat. Aliyah is very concerned about the quality and craft of the pie."

When the opportunity arose for this high school junior to take her baking skills into the large commercial kitchen at Uptown Kitchen to open her pie business, Aliyah jumped at the chance. "Kelly and Uptown Kitchen have been a big, big, big, help," she says. "I didn't know what to expect, and it was amazing. I remember the first time getting into the commercial kitchen—getting used to the equipment. That is a serious oven!"[34]

Producing her pies in the commercial kitchen at Uptown adds another level of professionalism and food safety to Aliyah's small business. Aliyah's mother explains:

> *Our products are made in a commercial kitchen—people can trust where they're made. It's not just a Cottage Food business. People are able to trust our name in the community and the label on our product. Our food is not only good, but it's also made in the right way—sanitary in a commercial kitchen. Word's out there in the community—"Aliyah is doing it right."*

In addition to food safety and technique, one of Aliyah's secrets is never compromising on the ingredients. "None of our pies have preservatives," says Aliyah. "I don't want to add chemicals to our pies to have a longer shelf life." She is a perfectionist and produces her goods in small batches with quality ingredients to ensure perfection. Aliyah is known to shop at the farmers' market for local eggs and butter—she swears it just makes her products better. Aliyah wants to ensure that all the ingredients are high quality, and she feels her commitment to choosing local ingredients helps her differentiate her product from others. "We get our eggs from S&S Lamb," she says proudly. "I could choose cheaper eggs, but I choose to buy eggs that just taste better and are local. And for butter—our butter in our baked goods and pies comes from Mooville and Cedarcrest. It is more expensive, but it's local and tastes better." Her mother supports her choices, noting, "We could have very well went and found everything at Meijer, but Aliyah wanted to keep things local. The eggs cost more, but they taste better. The better butter makes a better crust. The pecan pies are fluffier."

Aliyah sees opportunity to experiment with gluten-free crusts, vegan crusts and perfect crusts made with pastured pork lard. As a high school student at Forest Hills Northern, Aliyah is occupied by exams but looks ahead to her future after graduation. She hopes to expand her business and attend culinary school. "After high school, I might enroll in the GRCC culinary program," she says. Regardless of where Aliyah's career path will take her, Lysandra is very proud of her daughter, noting, "As a single mom, I try my best to encourage both my daughters to do their best. I am proud of her, and I'm excited to see her talents have a place to grow."

In addition to Uptown's commercial kitchen space, the location also boasts a dining room and demonstration kitchen. One of LeCoy's biggest clients, the Grand Rapids Cooking School, uses these facilities to offer uniquely tailored market-to-table food experiences—complete with a local market tour, cooking class and shared meal.

Begun by food entrepreneurs Molly Clauhs and Chris McKellar, the Grand Rapids Cooking School is now offering a full series of classes for the home chef. While the local Grand Rapids Community College culinary school offers programs for the culinary professional, the Grand Rapids Cooking School is geared toward the ever-growing popularity of getting back to the kitchen.

For Clauhs, mealtime is central to life and family, and the concept of "slow food" isn't anything new to her. Growing up, her mother ran a cooking school, and it was common for her mother to make five-course meals several times a week so that people would gather to "tuck into" large meals for several hours.[35]

Clauhs moved to Grand Rapids from upstate New York after graduating from Cornell in 2011. She hit the ground running to learn more about the local food community and immediately fell in love with the Eastown area's local charm. As the new girl on the street, Clauhs quickly made connections in the food community and, like LeCoy, landed an investment from DeVos's 5x5 to develop a business platform that quickly morphed into the Grand Rapids Cooking School.

At the same time, Clauhs acquired a former Salvation Army vehicle and created the Silver Spork, one of Grand Rapids' few food trucks. Clauhs keeps her focus on food that is simple, good tasting and locally focused. "People like our food because it's fresh and local," she says. The Silver Spork is only one of a few food trucks in town. Paul Lee's What the Truck was the first food truck to take to the streets in Grand Rapids in 2011. Along with What the Truck, the Silver Spork can be found at the farmers' markets and around town. The Silver Spork also focuses on catering farm dinners and private events for companies.

Like many other restaurateurs, Clauhs won't lie about the challenges of procurement. "It's hard work," she admits. "It's a lot of different people to purchase from, and it's a never-ending game." Clauhs procures her produce for the cooking school and the food truck at the Fulton Street Farmers' Market and from Farmlink, an extension of the local West Michigan Food Cooperative.

Whether it's Ben Bylsma's Real Food Farm tomatoes, Dancing Goat cheeses or Creswick's meats, it delights Clauhs to be able to create meals that both taste good and add to a strong local food system. "I have loved meeting and becoming friends with a network of local farmers and producers in West Michigan," she says. "It's a joy to buy their beautiful products, and I love knowing where my dollar is going."

Growing food artisans. *From left to right*: Rick DeVos, Aliyah French, Molly Clauhs and Kelly LeCoy. *Photo by Ryan Pavlovich.*

Clauhs's work gives her a chance to feel as though she's helping change American fast-food culture: "Life is short, and our communities are fragile. I believe in eating good, real food cooked from scratch. It simply feels right to me to eat locally—to know the people who grow or produce my food. I also feel comfortable building a business on that—it's something I'm proud of."

Chapter 5
Liquid Culture

We were the Sam Adams of Michigan micros. Our beers were well made, but they were unremarkable. It really wasn't until we made a decision to make great beer that everything turned around.
—Dave Engbers, Founders Brewing Co.

COFFEE

For twenty years, one coffee shop has been serving strong coffee and other house drinks and pastries to a loyal crowd. It's the neighborhood shops like the Kava House in Eastown that get the credit for being the early pioneers in the coffee-shop business in Grand Rapids. For many Grand Rapidians, the Kava House conjures up memories of late-night study dates or early mornings getting in line for a cup of strong, dark coffee.

In 1992, Kava House proprietress Leigh Vandermolen was fresh out of college at Michigan State and frequenting Café Royale in East Lansing. With no particular goal in mind for a career, Vandermolen thought about opening her own coffee shop. She and her mother, a recent empty nester, "rolled the dice and decided to start a business."[36] Vandermolen recalls:

> *Our search began in Eastown. I liked the feel of the area and thought the neighborhood would be accepting of our idea. Our original clientele was our wonderful neighbors, and the neighborhood really started to explode after we opened. In the beginning, we spent a lot of time simply educating our staff about what the heck a coffee house was. No one had ever seen an espresso machine before or tried to explain anything about the different beans or roasts.*

And twenty years later, the drink menu is nearly the same. There are now some new ingredients—soy milk, milk from local dairy farms, organic options and more homemade selections—because the customers are asking for it. For Vandermolen, however, the most important part isn't something that can be found on the menu. "My customers and staff have completely changed my life," she says. "They are so important to me—they are like family. I enjoy seeing everyone every day."

There so many variables that come into play when brewing the perfect cup of coffee, and while we may not be thinking about this complexity sip for sip, the coffee experts in Grand Rapids certainly are. To Chad Morton, co-owner of the Direct Trade Coffee Club, at the root of any coffee operation are the coffee farmers. It's Morton's main goal to develop a fair supply chain that is transparent and sustainable at every point along the line:

> *When I buy coffee, I go to the origin. We have direct-trade farms in Guatemala, Honduras and Costa Rica. It's beyond what's being labeled as "fair trade," which in some cases does not mean anything. It's direct trade, and it starts with the farmer. We have direct relationships with the farmers and growers, educating them on what we need in our coffee shop so that they can grow the best possible coffee. We then work with them to get them the best possible price for their high-value crop. Fair trade is not making the change in the marketplace as one might think. It's about direct trade—building a relationship with the farmer so he knows what to grow for the coffee buyer and how growing a quality bean will get him a higher price—something higher than what he could get from a wholesale buyer.[37]*

In a global agricultural economy, where coffee is the largest commodity crop traded, Morton feels people should come first:

People before profits…direct trade is not about charity; it's about empowering farmers. Roasters empower the farmers by offering payments based on the true quality of their crop. The higher the quality of the coffee, the more the roaster will pay for it. Creating a fair, equitable market in which coffee farmers can sell their coffee is at the core of social justice within the food system. Seeing small kids hauling large baskets of coffee cherries certainly makes you more willing to pay a few more cents a cup to make sure the farmer and his family get a fair wage. But high-quality coffee is always a must.

When the green coffee beans arrive in Grand Rapids, operations like Madcap Coffee roast them with patience and care under the right heat to bring out the perfect balance of flavors. This mindful roasting brings out the subtle characteristics of the coffee cherry. Ryan Knapp, Madcap roaster and barista, explains, "With great coffee, we are able to keep our roasts slightly lighter, allowing the inherent flavors to come through."[38] He also explains the drawbacks of the popular trend of heavier, dark-roasted coffees:

When coffee gets roasted really dark, the complex coffee flavor no longer comes through when you taste it. Rather, you begin to taste the smoky, woodsy notes that come from the roast. None of our roasts go very dark, as we want to make sure the customer can taste all the hard work that has gone into the coffee bean before it has reached our doorstep.

"Our baristas are coffee-focused culinary experts," says Knapp. "They know all of the coffee on our offering list—where they are from, who farmed them, what elevation it was grown, how it was processed and with what brew method the beverage would taste best."

Owner Trevor Corlett feels that Madcap is at the head of the national pack with its barista talent. "We're definitely striving to be the best at what we do," says Corlett.[39] "The success we've had at the barista competitions recently is a testament to the passion we have for coffee. Also, the competitions are a great opportunity for us to see how the coffees we are purchasing, and how we prepare them, stack up to what others in the industry are doing." He continues:

My goal from the start has been to provide my customers with a cup of coffee that, in a sip, can tell the "seed to cup" story. Our sole purpose is to offer the highest-quality coffee we can source. Our biggest challenge is educating our customers about coffee's "seed to cup" process, showing them

"Transfer Rate." Madcap Coffee. "Our baristas are coffee-focused culinary experts," says Madcap barista Ryan Knapp. "They know all of the coffee on our offering list—where they are from, who farmed them, what elevation it was grown, how it was processed and with what brew method the beverage would taste best." *Photo by Terry Johnston.*

the journey coffee takes before getting to their cups and how that journey affects the resulting taste.

And this coffee-focused culinary expertise is paying off. Madcap has a cult-like following of local foodies and creatives, and Madcap baristas' talents have earned them national recognition since the opening of the Grand Rapids shop. And with the addition of a second location in Washington, D.C., Madcap Coffee is now ranking among some of the best coffee institutions in the business. Knapp feels that across the United States, more and more people are giving attention to the quality of the coffee. "So often, coffee is seen as simply an afterthought, even in the highest levels of intentionality throughout the farm-to-table movement," he says. "I cannot tell you the number of times I've been at a well-respected restaurant and seen that they are serving poor coffee to pair with their delicious handcrafted desserts." But Knapp hopes to help change that. And with numerous barista and national awards under his belt, he assures us that he is not in it for the accolades. "I want to have fun and represent the coffee," he says. "That's what it's supposed to be about."

At the heart of it all, brewing coffee is a craft, much like making wine or beer. "Coffee is a craft,"[40] says Kurt Stauffer, the owner of Rowster New American Coffee. When you step foot into Stauffer's coffee shop, you step into a workshop. The son of a tradesperson himself, Stauffer has designed Rowster's coffee shop to have an aesthetic reminiscent of a craftsman's workbench, with repurposed industrial carts and tables with heavy woods and metal finishes. In the center of the coffee workshop is the roasting equipment, flanked on either side by brewing stations and the espresso dock. In the back, burlap sacks of beans sit against the wall and shelves, waiting to be brewed. Watching Stauffer and his staff work is to watch true artisans. Stauffer contemplates each varietal, deciding which one to put into the roaster that morning. The thoughtfulness of the bean, the brew and the customer experience is the result of Stauffer's passion for his work. His commitment to quality is his trademark.

Stauffer wasn't always in the coffee business. On his fortieth birthday, in the middle of his party, Stauffer got the call from his company—they were ceasing operations, and he was to be laid off. Effective immediately. "I just had a baby, I turned forty and my salary just disappeared." Stauffer was shell-shocked. "I was like, 'What the hell am I going to do with my life?'"

Stauffer began roasting coffee at home. Not sure what his next steps would be, he began offering his beans and brews in the back of the shop at the Richard App Gallery. And today, Stauffer's workshop—now very popular among foodies and neighborhood coffee seekers—is a reality that continues to evolve.

As a maker, Stauffer is extremely sentimental when he thinks about the history of Grand Rapids' productive past:

> *The thing about Grand Rapids…we've built good furniture, automotive parts. To me, it's important that we retain that connection to making things. Products need to be produced here. It's not some Silicon Valley boom-and-bust; it's about our community's self-sufficiency. It's alright. At least you had the chance to make something. This is what I said from day one when I opened Rowster.*

Stauffer remains committed to putting the craft back into making coffee. He and his business partner, Stephen Curtis, launched an online subscription service called Regular Coffee in 2012. Stauffer wants to put the good back into what we all do on a daily basis. Curtis and Stauffer are making something extraordinary regular. "Not everything can be, 'Come on in and spend three hours,'" says Stauffer. "We can give you something good and local and make it fast and easy. We want to be part of your everyday life. We are craft, not Kraft."

BUILDERS OF BEER CITY USA

Beer culture has always been a part of Grand Rapids' rugged history, but in the past decade, the craft-beer market has taken off. At the front of this movement, much credit goes to Founders Brewing Co. for setting the groundwork for the city that now holds the title of Beer City USA.

Dave Engbers, founding partner of Founders Brewing Co., looks over a bustling production facility. It looks like the line operation in the opening scene of the *Laverne and Shirley* sitcom. But that's where the similarities stop for this grass-roots-gone-global brewery.

The youngest of four children, Engbers was raised in Grand Rapids. "Food has always been a central part of our family's life," notes Engbers. "We had to be home after school because dinner would always be at six o'clock."[41] As for beer, Engbers remembers his dad only keeping the cheap stuff on the porch in the cooler. Engbers's first exposure to craft beer came when he spent time in California reconnecting with his estranged brother Chuck. It was 1986 in San Francisco. "Chuck introduced me to craft beer," recalls Engbers. "I had the Mendocino County Red Tail Ale, and I took one sip of that and was completely changed. It truly was an epiphany." When Engbers was nineteen years old, his parents bought him his first home-brew kit. "You would hang the bag, and there was a spigot. You'd add hot water and shake it and let it ferment. I can't even remember if we drank it," laughs Engbers.

During his time in college in the mid-90s, Engbers brewed beer and worked for a local distributor. He also met his future business partner, Mike Stevens, during this time, and this is where their dream to start a brewery came to be. Engbers and Stevens wanted to brew beer and be happy with their work. "The whole idea to start a brewery came about after the bar one night at three in the morning," recalls Engbers. "We realized that so many of our friends were graduating and not doing what they loved. No one was getting a job doing what they wanted."

After graduation, Engbers started teaching. "While I enjoyed teaching, all of the teachers at the school…so many of them were just waiting to retire," recalls Engbers. "They were burned out. And here I was, fresh out of college, ready to change the world." While teaching, Dave always had three batches of beer brewing on the weekends. "This is when I called Mike up and said, 'Let's go for it.' We are young enough that if it doesn't work, we can bounce back and do something else. Let's live without regrets."

The early craft-beer culture in Michigan was limited. "The only place you could really get other craft beers in Grand Rapids was Siciliano's on the West Side, Smitty's in Eastown and DW, but it was really hit or miss," recalls Engbers. "There wasn't a big market for craft beer then. Sometimes the beer was fresh, sometimes it was five months old." Engbers and Stevens wanted to change all that. The team developed a business plan, hired a brewer from upstate New York and started to lock in money with private investors and secure a location in which to open operations. Engbers remembers the late nights he spent looking for a safe locale that could house the brewpub. "At the time, Commerce was filled with prostitutes and drug dealers," he recalls. "There were cool buildings

A circa 1918 photograph showing Founders Brewing Co.'s first location, the Wolverine Brass Works building on 62–648 Monroe Avenue NW. *Photo courtesy of Grand Rapids Public Library.*

and architecture, but when I'd drive down there at 1:00 a.m., I knew it wouldn't be the best place for a pub—people would feel intimidated."

The team decided to investigate the dilapidated but historic Wolverine Brass Works building. Engbers recalls:

> We didn't need any keys; you could just walk in. It was wide open. I was so excited about it…natural old brick, wood floors—it was perfect. I took my family out to see it. We had to go into the alley and climb onto the chair. There were icicles on the first floor from a failed roof, and the floor was buckled. But we got in and saw how it could work. The taproom, the production, the bottling area—it was the beginning.

Founders began brewing with investors at their side, but the brewery was off its production target by 1,600 barrels. It wasn't looking promising for the new business. "We were hemorrhaging money," says Engbers. "Beer sales weren't where we thought they were going to be, and we were naive about the three-tier system in Michigan. We thought that if we made a good product at a reasonable price, everyone would buy it. Wrong. There were politics, personalities."

But there were also early champions of Founders beer. "There have been a lot of folks behind us—Siciliano's, International Beverage, Russo's, Martha's—all the locals," said Engbers. "The Gilmore Collection, with the B.O.B., they were an early supporter of our beer and having it on tap, as was Flannagan's and the Reptile House." Founders had the local backing, but Engbers had to diagnose the issue of the lacking sales:

> A bunch of craft beers were available, but everyone was doing the same thing. Everyone had a pale ale, an amber ale and an IPA. Everyone in Michigan was taking the lead from Larry Bell. Whatever he was doing seemed to work, so everyone was copying him. In an industry like this, you can't just copy. We needed to differentiate ourselves. We were the Sam Adams of Michigan micros. Our beers were well made, but they were unremarkable. It really wasn't until we made a decision to make great beer that everything turned around. We went for bigger, bolder, more complex and more aromatics. That's when we came up with a Scotch ale.

They called it Dirty Bastard, and it came just in time. Engbers notes:

> When we came out with Dirty Bastard, our business was in shambles. We hadn't paid our landlord in six months, and we hadn't paid our bank note

in probably four months. Our first brewer had left. He saw the writing on the wall that we were going to file for bankruptcy. His paycheck was bouncing, and I hadn't taken a paycheck in seven months. We brought in a few home brewers, and we said that from here on out, every beer was going to get bigger, bolder and more complex.

The new brewers were given free license to create bigger, bolder beers with more aromatics. "Never design a beer or create a recipe around cheap ingredients based on cost," said Engbers. "If there are better ingredients, we'll get them. If we need to charge more, we'll charge more. Two or three months later, we couldn't make beer fast enough." With this new creative license to brew what they believed was a solid set of beers, Founders created a whole new set of recipes.

Spurred on by a newfound confidence in their beers and fueled by the fear of failure, Founders got aggressive in road sales. Refusing to take no for an answer from retailers and wholesalers, Engbers sought to prove to the beer industry that Founders wasn't afraid to go bigger and bolder. "I knew our beers were better," says Engbers. "They were so delicious. I would do it in front of other brewers, and they'd say, 'Your beers aren't as hoppy as such and such,' and I'd say, 'Really?' And then I'd walk right behind the bar, pour one of their beers, put it right next to our beer and say, 'Here, try it.'"

Word was getting out about the Founders' Pale Ale, Curmudgeon, Breakfast Stout, Imperial and Devil Dancer. "We were creating beers that no one else was, and we instantly got the attention from beer enthusiasts," said Engbers. But they weren't out of the woods yet. Their accounting books were still in the red. "We had created a huge train wreck, and we still couldn't afford anything," Engbers recalls, "We'd buy grain, glass, cardboard—only the things that would keep us in business."

It was at the Extreme Beer Festival (EBF) where Founders finally got their break. An invite-only festival with breweries from both the West and East Coasts, the EBF gave Founders the chance to compete alongside top craft breweries across the country. "Every hour, we would tap a special beer," recalls Engbers. "Between the sessions, every brewer was hanging out with Founders. No one had ever heard of us, but our line was five times longer than anyone else's. All these breweries we had admired and looked up to were like, 'Who are you guys?' We were the unknown brewery. That weekend, we knew. Whatever we were doing was unique, but we needed to put the accelerator down—we needed to make money." Founders knew their beer was good, and they were customer focused. They kept their eyes on the industry reviews—Founders was earning national recognition. But the team was frustrated. "Life sucked," said Engbers, recalling how the bank owned their lives. "Those were the dark days, but we had a job to do. We picked ourselves up by our bootstraps and kept at it. We can look back on it now and say that we survived." It was the classic Midwest attitude.

With capacity at its limits, hindering their ability to get their accounting books into the black, the team looked to move out of the Brass Works building. "Our tanks were within centimeters of each other," recalls Engbers. "We simply didn't have room to grow at the Brass Works building. It was really only set up as a brewpub, and what we needed was an actual production facility."

And grow they did—into a building that had been sitting empty for years on Grandville Avenue. Built in the 1950s, the International Transfer Station was a loading dock where freight companies would load and consolidate their deliveries on their way to another destination. "When I walked into The Transfer Station, I knew it," recalls Engbers. "I could see it finished."

Engbers and Stevens kicked through the debris, which included some drug paraphernalia, porn, a used toilet and other garbage. "But we liked

Founders Brewing Co.'s second location was the Interstate System Shipping building on Grandville Avenue. *Photo courtesy of Founders Brewing Co.*

Above: Summertime at the Treehouse Community Garden. *Photo by Lisa Rose Starner.*

Left: Children harvesting new foods at a Grand Rapids school garden site. *Photo by Lisa Rose Starner.*

Author's food for thought. Questions must be asked: Who has access to good food—only those who can afford it? Where can it be found? Are the grocery stores that sell more affordable produce located in areas where people struggle in poverty? How are we going to help kids learn where their food comes from? And the growers—is starting a new farm possible for young people? What about fair wages for those people growing the food? What does it mean to try to make a fair food system for all? *Photo by Lisa Rose Starner.*

Backyard placemakers and local food activists. *Photo by Ryan Pavlovich.*

Grand Rapids City Commissioner Rosalyn Bliss—waiting for the city to hatch. *Photo by Ryan Pavlovich.*

The chicken whisperer. *Photo courtesy of Elizabeth and Andy DeBraber.*

Fresh greens at Uptown Farm. *Photo courtesy of Andy Dragt.*

A Jersey cow at the Lubbers Farm. *Photo courtesy of Karen Lubbers.*

Above: A greenhouse at the Trillium Haven Farm. *Photo by Shane Folkertsma.*

Right: Trillium's CSA shareholders harvesting potatoes. *Photo by Shane Folkertsma.*

Ben Bylsma's tomatoes at the Fulton Street Farmers' Market. *Photo by Jonathan Stoner.*

Tom Cary, farmer at Groundswell Farm, at the Fulton Street Farmers' Market. *Photo by Jonathan Stoner.*

Above: Anja Mast and Michael
VanderBrug, owners of Trillium
Haven Farm and Restaurant.
Photo by Jonathan Stoner.

Right: Bartertown founder
Ryan Cappelletti. *Photo by
Ryan Pavlovich*.

Left: Matthew Russell's Wednesday Evening delights, featured by vegan activist Adrienne Wallace. *Photo by Lynette Gram.*

Below: Nicolas Mika (left) has the vision to design a pop-up shipping container destination for food artisans in Grand Rapids. *Photo courtesy of MLive.*

Opposite, top: Farm-to-table cooking class at the Grand Rapids Cooking School. *Photo by Jonathan Stoner*; *Middle*: Molly Clauhs, owner of the Silver Spork food truck. A former Salvation Army vehicle, the Silver Spork is one of Grand Rapids' few food trucks. Clauhs keeps her focus on food that is simple, good-tasting and locally focused. *Photo by Stephanie Harding*; *Bottom*: Colombian coffee farmers. "Creating a fair, equitable market in which coffee farmers can sell their coffee is at the core of social justice within the food system," says coffee trader Chad Morton. *Photo by Chad Morton.*

A woman sorting coffee cherries in Guatemala. *Photo by Chad Morton.*

"Keepsake." Madcap Coffee. "My goal from the start has been to provide my customers with a cup of coffee that, in a sip, can tell the 'seed to cup' story," says Madcap owner Trevor Corlett. "Our sole purpose is to offer the highest-quality coffee we can source. Our biggest challenge is educating our customers about coffee's 'seed to cup' process, showing them the journey coffee takes before getting to their cups and how that journey affects the resulting taste." *Photo by Terry Johnston.*

Above: Kurt Stauffer of Rowster New American Coffee. *Photo by Ryan Pavlovich.*

Right: A bustling bottling facility at Founders Brewing Co. on Grandville Avenue. *Photo courtesy of Founders Brewing Co.*

Sietsema's Hard Cider in the orchard. *Photo courtesy of Andy Sietsema.*

New renovations have much improved the Fulton Street Farmers' Market. The redesign and development of the market in 2012 was very important to the immediate Midtown neighborhood. *Photo by Jonathan Stoner.*

The YMCA of Greater Grand Rapids Farmers' Market. *Photo courtesy of YMCA of Greater Grand Rapids.*

Ahavas community gardeners growing produce for the food pantry at Temple Emanuel. Each third week of the month, Temple Emanuel coordinates a food pantry distribution with the help of volunteers, converting the synagogue's multipurpose room into a "shop" for area residents. *Photo courtesy of Ahavas Israel.*

Left: Gleaning at a nearby farm for the Feeding America West Michigan food bank. Feeding America West Michigan is doing more and more to reclaim the excess of not just large food suppliers but also locally grown fresh food and vegetables. The organization has a steady stream of conventional produce from across the country—from tomatoes to fruits to melons—as they come into season in their different growing regions. But director Ken Estelle is most proud of the food bank's efforts to connect with local growers to reclaim local food for the food bank system. *Photo courtesy of Feeding America West Michigan.*

Right: The future. "Teaching kids how to feed themselves and how to live in a community responsibly is the center of an education." —Alice Waters. *Photo by Lisa Rose Starner.*

Below: The West Michigan Academy for Environmental Science, where the classroom is the outdoors, is located just outside downtown Grand Rapids. The acreage surrounding the school is home to a variety of ecosystems that Holly Orions uses for teaching, including a wetlands area, woods, a bit of prairie and a cultivated community garden complete with a greenhouse, chickens and a mud oven. *Photo courtesy of West Michigan Academy for Environmental Science.*

Opposite, bottom: Building raised beds at the Baxter Community Center greenhouse. *Photo courtesy of Baxter Community Center.*

Above: Students at West Michigan Academy for Environmental Science grow over 30 percent of what they eat in their salad bar. *Photo courtesy of West Michigan Academy for Environmental Science.*

Left: Growing hope at the Treehouse Community Garden. *Photo by Lisa Rose Starner.*

Founders Brewing Company today. *Photo courtesy of Founders Brewing Co.*

what we had to work with," Engbers recalls. "We liked the garage doors, and we could see an expanded deck. We took a garden hose that was lying there, stretched it out and used it to mark where a serpentine bar would be. Then we used empty CO_2 tanks to mark out the pool table, railings and stage. In about ten minutes, we had our floor plan drawn up, ready to give to the architect. That's literally how that came about."

The new facility would allow Founders to ramp up production each year by leaps and bounds, but the move wasn't without anxiety. Engbers knew they had to double their sales to break even. "I had nothing to back me up, just a gut feeling," he recalls. "I felt that we couldn't make beer fast enough and that this move would solve the issue." Fortunately, the numbers proved him right. In 2008, after a year at the new location, Founders had sold 10,000 barrels. Sales increased dramatically. They sold 19,000 barrels in 2009, and the number kept going up each year. Founders predicts sales of 135,000 barrels in 2013. Today, Founders is the fastest-growing brewery in the United States, and in both 2010 and 2011, it was the highest-rated brewery in the world.

Founders Brewing Co. is finally paying the bills. Their books are in the black, and they've become world famous. They have also managed to keep the local brewpub feel. "Everyone's welcome. It doesn't matter your color, who you are sleeping with, Democrat or Republican. Leave your title at the door," Engbers declares.

For the beer enthusiasts, the Tap Room is the brewers' playground. "We learn pretty quickly what people like or don't like," says Engbers. "They are our extended Founders' family, and they are pretty vocal about what we have on tap. It's virtually immediate feedback." As they grow, Engbers recognizes the trends and the novelties but has only one focus for their beers: quality. "We don't put anything in the beer if it doesn't add to the quality of the beer," he notes. "We won't compromise, and we invest in new technologies, equipment, ingredients and people. Everything we do will make our beer better."

Engbers and Stevens's drive and hunger are still evident in their business today. Their grit, ingenuity and dedication helped put Grand Rapids on the beer map, fermenting the way for other aspiring craft-beer entrepreneurs to follow their passion in the industry.

Even with Founders' growth and increase in production, Engbers knows that there is still tremendous room for growth in the American craft-beer market. Annual consumption of craft beer in the United States is quite low, hovering between 3 to 5 percent. Engbers feels that Founders, in partnership with other breweries, can help continue to grow the consumer's palate, driving those sales up over the next ten years. Founders finds motivation in other breweries launching fresh recipes. "We don't compete head to head with other brewers, and we like to see new breweries come up through the ranks and gain recognition," says Engbers. "There is great beer being brewed here and everywhere around the world."

As Founders continues to grow, the owners want to maintain the culture, vision and philosophy of the business while encouraging the growth of the craft industry around Grand Rapids. "We do this because we're passionate about it, and we enjoy being able to share it with other people," notes Engbers. "We get to come to work and do what we love, and other brewers are in the same boat. We've grown this cottage industry together. Many of us have gone throughout the same struggles—financing, hard work, demanding schedules—and we love it."

Following in Engbers and Stevens's footsteps are entrepreneurs Mark and Michelle Sellers, owners of BarFly Ventures. The two met while living in Chicago. They moved to Grand Rapids in 2007, just ahead of the economic downturn, to launch HopCat, the area's first beer bar. Mark, with his entrepreneurial spirit, wanted to leave the financial industry and go out on his own. Michelle took a leap of faith, and together they jumped from Chicago into the Grand Rapids market with the idea to launch a beer bar. The Sellers wrote their business plan on a napkin while traveling through Europe exploring brewpubs for concepts for their own beer bar.

HopCat is now known worldwide as one of the top beer bars on the planet, as listed in *BeerAdvocate* magazine. Within six months, the couple went from business plan to blueprint to buildout, and HopCat, featuring their own brews alongside local and national favorites, was opened in 2008. It subsequently turned a profit its first year and has since received numerous accolades for its brews.[42]

In 2012, the Sellers decided to take another step in progressing the craft-brew scene in Grand Rapids. The task? Reinvent the Grand Rapids Brewing Company (GRBC). "We knew it had been struggling and that they were looking for a buyer," said Michelle. "Mark had always had his eye on it. It has a lot of history—a venerable name with a great pedigree."

Grand Rapids Brewing Company's horse-drawn delivery wagon with drivers, circa 1915. At its peak, GRBC was brewing 250,000 barrels of beer for the city of Grand Rapids. *Photo courtesy of Grand Rapids Public Library.*

The Grand Rapids Brewing Company is significant in the history of Grand Rapids' brew culture. The first of the Grand Rapids breweries was opened in 1836 by Englishman John Pannell. This along with four other breweries would eventually make up the Grand Rapids Brewing Company. In 1847, Christopher Kusterer opened the second of the four breweries. Z.Z. Lydens notes of the times, "In 1847, chills and shaking ague were terrors of malarially afflicted people. In the eight years following came two experiences—a great growth in the habit of drinking lager beer and an almost complete dying out of the shaking ague."[43]

At its peak, GRBC was brewing 250,000 barrels of beer for the city of Grand Rapids. In 1918, Prohibition forced the brewery to stop production and change its name to Grand Rapids Products Co.[44] The Grand Rapids Brewing Company wasn't to begin beer production again until 1935. With this history in mind, the Sellers were determined to bring the GRBC away from its flailing post on Twenty-eighth Street and give it a place deserving of its iconic history back in the central city, right on the corner of Ionia and Fulton, next to the popular Van Andel Arena. To create a space deserving of the brand, BarFly brought on local architectural firm Lott3Metz to design a space that celebrated Grand Rapids' rich downtown architectural history. Much of the materials used were reclaimed, including floor joists from the original building. The Grand Rapids Brewing Company—a brand once on the brink of becoming defunct—is now one of the pioneers in the craft-brew industry, having gained status as a certified organic brewery. The three brewers on staff are highly focused on using quality, organic-certified ingredients for their classic recipes, as well as new brews on tap.

While many local breweries procure their hops from out of state, GRBC procures its hops from New Mission Organics, a twenty-acre hop farm in Leelanau County. Owned by Brian Tennis, New Mission Organics has over twenty different varieties of certified-organic hops that are grown especially for Grand Rapids Brewing Company. The brewers have found that using these ingredients increases quality in the end production. As Grand Rapids Brewing Company exposes more and more people to their high-quality products, they hope that it catalyzes other hop and grain farms and malteries to expand their crops and turn to organic farming. GRBC's food menu complements their beer, using as many local ingredients as possible. Creating classic pub fare rustic in presentation, the kitchen takes time to create good food that is based on as many local producers as possible.

As for the waste, the spent organic grain from GRBC's brewing process is passed along to the organic dairy farmers at Grassfields Cheese as part

Grand Rapids Brewing Company's new home in downtown Grand Rapids at Ionia and Fulton. *Photo courtesy of Barfly Ventures.*

of their composting program. Grassfields, which also supplies the brewery's restaurant with its cheeses, uses the grains as feed filler for its pastured cows to help bridge the gap between grass seasons. Both brewer and farmer feel that these practices not only are vertically integrated and truly sustainable but also create lasting relationships in the food system. The process has integrity and stands alone in the local food industry.[45]

Sellers believes that the more people that can be recruited into the craft beer industry the better. "There is room for all of us—Harmony, Vivant, Founders, Perrin—all of the growing breweries," he says. "No one is throwing elbows in each other's ribs. We are helping to build each other's business. It's fraternal." Brewery Vivant, Harmony and Perrin are several other breweries making their permanent mark on the craft-beer scene in Grand Rapids. Home brewers Dave Petroelje and Tyler Nickerson hope to jump in on the trend as they speculate on their own potential beer business. "Businesses like Founders and HopCat—they've cleared the way for us smaller guys," Nickerson explains.[46] Petroelje and Nickerson, both committed Grand Rapids residents, see potential in the market and have brewing talents that can add value to the growing scene. "And then there is Brewery Vivant, who started small and just kept growing," says

Nickerson. "We have a lot of pioneers here in our city, and that is good for us as a new business."

Amy Sherman, local food advocate and host of the Grand Rapids–produced *Great American Brew Trail*, looks back on her own times as a home brewer in the upstairs of her Eastown college apartment. "I was brewing beer way back in 1993 and '94," she recalls, "just when Bell's opened and Samuel Adams started distributing the first craft brews."[47] Sherman worked at Grand Rapids Brewing Company when it was located on Twenty-eighth Street and remembers being laughed at for moving from Detroit to Grand Rapids:

> *When I moved from Detroit, Grand Rapids was the place where the carpets rolled up at 7:00 p.m. Now it's all very different, and I enjoy watching the city grow. I've really been a part of the birth of a city…we keep chipping away at it regardless of the status quo. The cool stuff has happened at the grass roots, community level. It hasn't been forced, and it has soul.*

Of her PBS documentary on Michigan's craft breweries, Amy says that it's all a labor of love: "It's all about fun and promoting Michigan beer and the artists who brew it," she says. "This is a Michigan craft."

FROM ROOTSTOCK TO BOTTLE

The craft culture isn't happening only in the areas of beer and coffee—Grand Rapids–made cider is also beginning to see its time in the sun. Across the country, apple growers are faced with challenges that include unpredictable weather patterns, global apple competition with countries like China and labor issues. To remain competitive and reach an additional market, they are tapping into the local artisanal movement by turning to pressing their orchard's apples into hard cider.

Grand Rapids has a history of local cideries, but fourth-generation apple farmer Andy Sietsema is looking to take cider to a whole new level of quality and perfection. On his sixty acres of orchards just outside the city, Sietsema cultivates over one hundred varieties of heirloom apples. He wants the country to know that there's more out there than just Macintosh and Honeycrisp.

Sietsema's relationship with the land goes back several generations. "My great-grandfather was in real estate, and during the Great Depression, he

The Sietsema family apple business has been in Grand Rapids for four generations. *Photo courtesy of Andy Sietsema.*

bought all the land our orchards sit on," he notes. "And then his children, my dad and now me—we are all apple growers. I was always told my great-grandfather was a really good guy."[48]

Out in the orchard, Sietsema walks past his rootstock beds. He can identify nearly any apple by its skin, aroma and flesh. He has an intimate relationship with both the land and the apples that he's trying to bring back into cultivation. "We have over 110 varieties out in the field," he says proudly.

Over 150 years ago, there were over fourteen thousand varieties of apples in the United States. Now only a handful of commercial varieties are available at the supermarket. "There are a few of us growing heirlooms," reports Sietsema. "The naysayers say there is no money in heirloom table apples. I say, 'bull.' I can get more money for heirloom table apples than I can for Honeycrisps. I've got a list of restaurants knocking down my door that want heirloom table apples for serving with cheese plates and for cooking."

When you walk into Sietsema's cider winery, the smell of crisp apples fill the air. It's similar to the smells that grapes give to wine country—sweet, fermenting fruit. Over at the fermenting tanks, Sietsema gets excited talking about the different yeasts he's tried. "They are all champagne yeasts," he notes. "Cider is not a beer; it's a wine." Sietsema's small winery license allows him to sell and distribute. "We can sell to restaurants and straight out of the tasting room. I have no shortage of people who want it. Many restaurants want it on tap, but I don't have the full capacity right now to get it all over town."

Sietsema's quality cider is winning accolades from experts and drinkers alike. Then there are the pies. "Other places are buying their pies and reselling them as part of the experience," reveals Sietsema. "They say home baked, not homemade. Our pies are homemade."

Siciliano's, Grand Rapids' specialty retailer for home-brewing supplies, has helped grow the trend of craft beer and cider with its shop. Weston Eaton points out that "craft beer is by definition less about market share and more an expression of a new identity—one premised on small-scale, authentic and traditional methods of production."[49] Eaton notes that "craft beer is a social movement whose boundaries are porous, aims are fluid and champions are varied and contested. And one in which we, as home or professional brewers or industry folk or especially as beer drinkers, can have a hand in steering." In the end, Eaton advocates that as the community expands its artisanal offerings, the movement needs to to stay true to quality and avoid watering down the "local" brand. Place matters.[50]

Chapter 6

To Market, To Market: Markets for a Twenty-First-Century Food System

Public markets are the essence of place. The markets draw people together and provide a universal shopping experience wherein all of humanity can be found. Public markets, neighborhood markets, grocery stores and specialty shops meld together the smells and flavors of a community. Throughout the course of its history, Grand Rapids has relied on the merchants and market places to keep its people fed. Today, there is a resurgence of farmers' markets and locally owned retailers hoping to re-create access to fresh foods within the urban neighborhoods, making these neighborhoods more livable and vibrant.

FARMERS' MARKETS

In May 2012, city leaders and food advocates cut the ribbon on the newly renovated Fulton Street Farmers' Market (FSFM). The redesign and development of the market in 2012 was very important to the immediate

Leonard Street Produce Market, circa 1930. *Photo courtesy of Grand Rapids Public Library.*

Midtown neighborhood. Fulton Street Farmers' Market is there first and foremost to ensure that the local residents have access to fresh, healthy foods. "This was originally a neighborhood market," said Christine Helms-Maletic, director of the FSFM. "We wanted to make sure people understand that, and we want to keep it that way, particularly by making sure that we serve the low-income families in the immediate neighborhood by providing access to fresh, healthy, affordable and local food."

In the 1920s, FSFM began as a grassroots effort among families when food prices were beginning to soar. The markets at the time were primarily wholesale, and the retail market was borne out of the idea of neighbors making fresh fruits and vegetables accessible to families. "Ninety years later, it is very cool to see that Fulton Street Farmers' Market remains a neighborhood market run by a group of leaders that live in the neighborhood," says Helms-Maletic. "It isn't led by the city. The values are the same today as they were ninety years ago."[51]

At its core, Helms-Maletic describes the renovation of the market as first and foremost a neighborhood improvement project to bring vitality to the immediate neighborhood:

> *We wanted to preserve and restore this neighborhood asset. The market was literally falling apart. We were concerned that vendors were going to*

Fulton Street Farmers' Market, 1922. *Photo courtesy of Fulton Street Farmers' Market.*

start to go elsewhere and that the neighborhood would be without access to quality food. And as the market is owned by the city, budgets were also a concern—we were worried that the continued budget pressures could be the demise of the market.

Serious talks about renovation began in the mid-2000s, as the popularity of local foods was continuing to grow. Local food advocates Tom Cary and Jayson Otto were at the forefront of these conversations to preserve the Fulton Street Farmers' Market. "These two individuals were asking the serious questions about the future of this market, says Helms-Maletic. "They were kicking ideas around and asking 'How can we make it sustainable for the next twenty years? How can this help catalyze neighborhood redevelopment? How will this be a center for a fair and just twenty-first-century food system?'"

There was also a high degree of suspicion among the farmers early on in the renovation project. "What will they do with the market? They don't know anything about running a farmers' market," Helms-Maletic recalls the farmers saying early on in the planning. Helms-Maletic attributes early successes to neighborhood leader Jayson Otto for managing these complex pieces. "He built trust between the farmers, neighbors, vendors and the neighborhood association," she says.

Market organizers intentionally focused on increasing the local traffic to the market. Helms-Maletic recalls:

We kept asking, "Why is it that our customers are coming from five miles away? How do we increase our local users?" There seemed to be a perception by neighbors that the market wasn't for them—that it was too expensive. They felt it was only for whites, for yuppies. You could look around…it was not a diverse customer base or vendor base. But now the diversity is increasing.

Helms-Maletic attributes the increase in socio-economic diversity to their intentional focus on making the market appeal to the immediate neighborhood—letting them know that the foods available there were affordable and that food-benefit programs like Bridge Cards, WIC coupons and Project Fresh could all be used at the market to purchase fresh, local food. The director observed a measurable increase in the usage of these benefits. Between 2009 and 2010, FSFM tripled the use of Bridge Cards, WIC coupons and Project Fresh. Then, in 2011, the use tripled again, and then again in 2012, when benefits were matched with a community program called Double Up Food Bucks, which allowed customers to double their assistance monies for fresh food purchases at the markets. "These are the results of trying to make it more appealing to the people here in the central-city neighborhoods," said Helms-Maletic.

But as a neighborhood market, the Fulton Street Farmers' Market has only so much reach in the community. Helms-Maletic sees complementary roles between the FSFM and the new Downtown Market. "The Downtown Market will be complementary to what is growing here at Fulton Street," explains Helms-Maletic. "The Downtown Market serves a completely different function and could be the convener for the hard food systems issues. It has that potential in so many more ways to be a regional food hub, but it won't be like the Fulton Street Farmers' Market—the neighborhood farmers' market."

Spearheaded by Grand Action, a powerful local economic development corporation, the Downtown Market has been a dream in the making for over five years. The Downtown Market, opening July 2013, will be a four-season indoor/outdoor public market, complete with a teaching greenhouse, children's kitchen, commercial food business space, event space and even a brewery/distillery.

Grand Action's past projects include large-scale developments such as the Van Andel Arena. With the Downtown Market, Grand Action has brought large stakeholders to the table to create market programming, connecting the dots between local food and healthcare, education and culinary arts education. Because of the potential for the programming at Downtown Market, food systems experts are calling it a "regional food hub" in the making and a significant addition to the local food system.[52]

Ted Spitzer, consultant for the Downtown Market, is hopeful:

Conceptual sketch of the Downtown Market, which is set to open in the summer of 2013. *Sketch courtesy of Grand Action.*

The Downtown Market can bring together people from all facets of the food community. It is a place where tough issues like food justice and policy issues can be brought to a more broad community, which will help move forward these issues in a way that Grand Rapids has not been able to do up to this point. Just the bringing people together will provide a pathway to talk about these problems and can help launch solutions to our broken food system.

However, not everyone is so sure that the Downtown Market will be able to deliver on its promises for attacking the larger food systems issues within Grand Rapids. Food justice advocates like Lisa Oliver-King of Our Kitchen Table remain skeptical. "The [current local] food system primarily benefits communities with racial and economic privileges—e.g. the new Downtown Market—and many restaurants that working-class people cannot afford," says Oliver-King. "There is a lack of real community involvement and input, and a small number of experts and usual suspects are making decisions for everyone else. Expanding markets into underserved areas of the community is necessary if we are going to address social justice issues and create a fair food system that is accessible to everyone."[53]

But Oliver-King finds hope in the fact that smaller farmers' markets have also popped throughout city—from the Westside, to Plainfield, to the Southeast Community Association—all of which have been helpful in meeting fresh-food-access needs. Other organizations are also investing in farmers' markets around the community. As part of its wellness program, the YMCA of Grand Rapids has an on-site farmers' market. And in order to serve those not able to make it to the market, it took to the streets with the Veggie Van.

In its second year, the Veggie Van serves as a mobile farmers' market to areas deemed as "food deserts"—areas lacking a steady supply of fruits and vegetables. "Parents are often thrilled to purchase fresh produce using their Bridge Cards or WIC, especially since so little fresh food is available in the core city," said YMCA coordinator Julie Sielawa.[54] "And residents of senior housing centers such as Delaware Manor are thrilled that our Veggie Van stops right at their front door."

Since the program's launch, the YMCA has seen a great response from families who have been using the Veggie Van for their source of fresh, local and nutritious food. "It's exciting when kids from schools like Cesar Chavez or Martin Luther King Elementary line up after school to spend their quarters on apples or bags of grapes," says Sielawa. "On a typical week, we have about fifteen vendors [at the on-site farmers' market at the downtown YMCA]. Many of these same farmers also supply produce for the Veggie Van and have been grateful for the opportunity to sell what they grow year-round. This past summer, kids who grew produce at YMCA community gardens were able to build entrepreneurial skills by selling produce at the market, and we plan to expand that effort this coming year."

Local hospitals are also beginning to offer weekly farmers' markets for their employees and immediate neighborhood residents. Metro Health Hospital was one of the first hospitals to adopt an on-site farmers' market, and St. Mary's Healthcare and Spectrum Health Hospitals have developed their own markets as well.

Sarah Chartier organizes the Spectrum Health Farmers' Market at the downtown medical center. "Our focus on access includes a farmers' market at our downtown medical center," explains Chartier.[55] "In the most recent year, we trialed a free bussing system for the local community and provided EBT access, Double Up Food Bucks and weekly healthy cooking demonstrations."

The Spectrum Health Farmers' Market was initiated after Spectrum's director of facilities visited another hospital's on-site farmers' market. "Beyond the farmers' market, we also hold annual Community Supported Agriculture programs for staff at multiple locations," explains Chartier. "At our South Pavilion campus, we built an inclusive community garden for staff and patients. The garden is visible from the physical therapy area and was built so that those with physical restrictions are able to participate."

Spectrum Health is also working to increase local food purchasing for their food service. "We have signed the Healthy Food in Health Care Pledge and the Healthy Food Hospital Campaign," says Chartier. "In general, supporting local food purchasing directly supports local farmers and the community financially, increases food security and decreases the carbon footprint of our food purchases."

GROCERY RETAILERS

At one time in Grand Rapids history, small grocery retailers supplied neighborhoods with everything residents needed—from fresh foods to pantry staples. There were no big-box chain stores and discount chain retailers. That was the urban experience.

The Alger Market, located at 2413 Eastern SE, May 1954. At one time in Grand Rapids history, small grocery retailers supplied neighborhoods with everything residents needed—from fresh foods to pantry staples. *Photo courtesy of the Grand Rapids Public Library.*

As farmers' markets are innovating to reach new markets, grocery retailers must also reconsider their locations and offerings to help increase access to quality fresh fruits and vegetables around the city. Where it was once common to have family-owned grocers on every corner in every neighborhood, today, sadly, the core city lacks the same variety of produce, and many outlets are higher in cost than the grocers located in the suburban periphery of the city.

Longtime Italian specialty grocer and retailer John Russo remembers when South Division was primarily composed of Italian immigrants, with his own immigrant family's small neighborhood-based grocery in Grand Rapids serving the neighborhood. "I am the fourth generation of our family to live and work [in this business]," explains Russo, who now owns Carrettino Italian Market Wine. "My grandfather, the late G.B. Russo, came by himself to Grand Rapids at seventeen years old in 1902. He did a lot of hard manual labor in order to save enough money to bring his parents and siblings here from our native Montelepre, Sicily. People from Sicily, Lebanon and Greece were arriving here in the late 1800s and early 1900s. Most were settling in the neighborhood along South Division, bounded by Wealthy and Hall Streets."[56]

And it was on South Division—746 to 752 South Division at Franklin—where the Russo family business served the Italian and other Mediterranean immigrants, providing them with the groceries and foods of their homeland. Russo recalls:

> *The unit at 752 South Division was where the G.B. Russo & Son International Grocery was located from 1908 to 1967. G.B. Russo & Son was moved to 1935 Eastern SE in 1967 to 1976. Then we were able to acquire property on Twenty-ninth Street to build the present location. My brother Joe M. Russo and I worked very hard to build that business into a premier specialty food and wine store.*

Russo envisions his children continuing the family tradition, serving as grocers to the local community. "Since we opened Carrettino, I have sent

G.B. Russo & Son International Grocery, located at 752 South Division Street, served Grand Rapids residents from 1908 until 1967. *Photo courtesy of John Russo.*

my son Greg to Italy twice," he notes. "We have plans for a lot of wonderful food and wine products that we will introduce to West Michigan over the next few years. The foundation of the business is well planned for. My three eldest kids, Gina, Mike and Greg, have been involved in the business many years and are quite capable of carrying it on for a long time to come."

Today, there are many Spanish *mercados* that supply the Hispanic neighborhoods with traditional foods, while the Asian markets supply the various Asian communities south of Grand Rapids. Specialty grocers like Carrettino, as well as other specialty food retailers like Martha's Vineyard, Art of the Table, Kingma's Market and Siciliano's, offer a plethora of options for artisan foodstuffs and specialty groceries. However, there is still a need for full-service supermarkets and grocery stores throughout Grand Rapids, particularly in the downtown areas, to fill the gaps where local residents may not have access to good, healthy food.

Eberhard's Foods, 1526 Plainfield Avenue NE, Grand Rapids, June 5, 1948. Where it was once common to have family-owned grocers on every corner in every neighborhood, today, sadly, the core city lacks the same variety of produce, and many outlets are higher in cost than the grocers located in the suburban periphery of the city. *Photo courtesy of Grand Rapids Public Library.*

Grand Rapids has no shortage of local supermarket chains. DW, Spartan Stores and Meijer Inc. are all regionally based in the Greater Grand Rapids area and have stores located throughout the area. However, the majority of these stores (particularly those carrying a premium selection of fresh and affordable foods) are located beyond Grand Rapids' city center, following the trend of suburban development.

The displacement of food retailers to the periphery of the city has created several unintended consequences. In addition to being an inconvenience to downtown residents, most urban residents, particularly those urban poor, do not have widespread access to a diverse range of fruits and vegetables at an affordable price. Even though there is an economic push toward redevelopment within the central downtown, the economics for these larger chains to invest in small stores within the central city areas still don't add up. According to downtown development advocates, "The amount of square footage, the number of on-site parking spaces and the current number of residents in the central business district cause [retail grocery] developers to struggle when putting together a cost-effective development."[57]

The issue with a lack of access to nutritionally-sound food in Grand Rapids' urban areas has caught the attention of public health advocates, who are choosing to step in where the market is seemingly failing to meet this need. Because of the impact on public health and diet-related chronic disease, Michigan State University Medical School and Blue Cross Blue Shield are also working to transform urban convenience stores into healthy food stores that community residents across Grand Rapids can access. Working together with Neighborhood Ventures, a community economic development organization funded by the W.K. Kellogg Foundation, "healthy corner stores"[58] are being piloted as strategies to increase access to fresh, healthy foods. This initiative, dubbed the "Health Corner Store Network," aims to support convenience stores to stock and sell healthier items and provides meaningful marketing materials for healthy foods. A partnership with the YMCA's Veggie Van helps the convenience stores stock local produce on their shelves. The project seeks to engage the local shop owners and help them build capacity to pursue and continue a healthy corner-store business model. Ultimately, the network wants to see these efforts make an impact on the obesity epidemic that is rampant in urban areas.

Sheri Rop, shopkeeper and owner of Nourish Organic Market, sees and understands the issue related to food access across the city. Rop comes from a local good-food background. Having worked with on-farm retail operations at Grassfields Farm and Trillium Haven Farm, Rop is solidly committed to supporting organic farmers doing the right things for the land, the food and the people and offering those selections in her urban store.

Nourish Organic Market is centrally located in the Wealthy Street corridor and strives to serve the immediate low-income neighborhood. However, Rop admits to struggling with the issues of cost and access. "Organic food costs more," she notes. "That's the cost of real food that is properly grown. The farmers that are growing it are barely making a living."[59] Rop wants to increase access to fresh, healthy foods in her community. "We partner with Baxter Community Center in as many ways as we can," she says. "And of course, finding ways to get people with limited financial resources who are already interested in organic food better access to it is very important to us." Rop's store also accepts Bridge Cards. "We have taken Bridge Cards from the beginning, but I'm very dissatisfied by the proportion of our sales to Bridge Card holders," says Rop. "We need to find ways to do a lot better in this area."

Rop hopes her store will help fill a void but believes that there are other components, such as education, that need to be addressed. "My primary interest in working on the broader issue would be with gardening and cooking efforts," she says. "This seems to be the most effective way of changing people's perceptions and understandings about food."

Chapter 7

Setting a Place at the Table: Ensuring Good Food for All

The first thing you have to do is get into your kitchen. Get in your kitchen and get jazzed up about learning and cultivating the domestic culinary arts.
—Farmer Joel Salatin on fighting industrial agriculture[60]

The Greater Grand Rapids area has a tremendous reputation for its nonprofit work and prides itself on its dedication to ensuring quality of life for its citizens—whether that be helping a person locate suitable work, receive food from an emergency shelter or navigate the social services network for healthcare assistance. Many of the social services delivered within the Grand Rapids community are coordinated through houses of worship, which have served as the front lines of support services for people in their communities. For many, a church, synagogue or mosque is the first place one would go to ask for help, as these are safe, trustworthy environments.

Offering emergency food assistance is only a piece of solving the food security issue in our communities. It is not a long-term solution, and it does not change the foundations of the broken industrialized food system or help move people toward food independence. Concepts such as cooking classes,

Radishes. *Photo by Shane Folkertsma.*

community gardens, seed saving and foraging are foundational life skills that can restore people's ability to feed themselves and the tools they need to do it with good, healthful food.

HELPING WITH HUNGER

Now the director of operations, Barb Duchemin has been involved with the food pantry at Temple Emanuel for over fifteen years. When Duchemin stepped in, the temple's pantry was serving only fifteen families. "We serve the broader community, and we see the needs continue to grow," explains Duchemin. "In today's times, people really rely on the pantry for their food. Food stamps have been cut, and people have lost employment benefits. I see it as a real necessity in helping keep people afloat."[61] Temple Emanuel is one of many faith-based institutions operating within the faith-based ACCESS pantry network, which includes over sixty food pantries in the area and organizes food drives and manages client referrals. Duchemin believes that the ACCESS network can help people negotiate their way through what is a very complicated social-services system.

Each third week of the month, Duchemin coordinates the pantry distribution with the help of volunteers, converting the synagogue's multipurpose room into a "shop" for area residents. The setup provides a grocery-store experience for the pantry clients, who can shop around in different stations to collect cans of food, dry goods, frozen meats and fresh vegetables. A sister synagogue, Ahavas Israel, maintains a community garden where a large portion of the bounty is offered to Temple Emanuel's pantry as a source of additional fresh fruits and vegetables.

Duchemin is a physician's assistant at a local health clinic and knows the importance of the role of fresh fruits and vegetables as part of a healthy diet. "Most of the diseases and chronic illness I see in my patients can be managed in part with a healthier diet," she explains. At the pantry, Duchemin sees the reality of health disparities that exist because of poverty. "Education about diet choices and access are among the biggest barriers for people in choosing and preparing healthier meals for themselves," says Duchemin. "Health starts in the kitchen." Duchemin envisions additional cooking classes that tie in seasonal foods, and she has received a grant from Feeding America to start to realize this vision. "I would like to reach out and see if my clients are willing to come to a class with cooking lessons or gardening lessons," says Duchemin. But for now, she wants to add in simple strategies, such as "giving recipes to clients when we have fresh vegetables. People will look at it and say, what is this? What do I do with it? Sadly, it's easier for some people to just open the can or box."

Like many other ACCESS food pantries, Duchemin's pantry benefits from the food resources gleaned by Feeding America West Michigan. Formerly known as Second Harvest Gleaners, Feeding America West Michigan is one of Michigan's largest food banks, reclaiming and redistributing over 2 million pounds of food a month to over 1,300 charitable agencies like Temple Emanuel.[62]

Located on the outskirts of the city in an industrial park, Feeding America West Michigan continues to work to meet its goal of ending hunger under the direction of Ken Estelle. The warehouse is a bustling operation, with staff and volunteers hurrying in and out of the facility directing and redirecting the food product and produce. The food bank is responsible for the recovery, procurement and redistribution of the glut that is found within the industrial food system. Feeding America West Michigan's top food product donors are Wal-Mart and Kraft Foods.

A driving force in the development of the food bank was the late Jon Arnold. A passionate man, resolute to put an end to hunger in West Michigan and across the country, Arnold believed that it was possible to end hunger within West Michigan, given all the resources within the industrial food system. From product overruns and supply surpluses, Arnold believed it was a distribution issue—not a supply issue—that allowed hunger to exist in the West Michigan community. He set out to create solutions to get these resources to the people who needed it most. He fought and worked toward this goal until his death in 2011, serving tirelessly as an advocate for the hungry in West Michigan.

Feeding America West Michigan is doing more and more to reclaim the excess of not just large food suppliers but also locally grown fresh food and vegetables. The organization has a steady stream of conventional produce from across the country—from tomatoes to fruits to melons—as they come into season in their different growing regions. But Estelle is most proud of the food bank's efforts to connect with local growers to reclaim local food for the system.[63]

Gavin Orchards is one partner farm that is teaming up with the food bank to ensure a steady supply of fresh food for the pantries. Gavin Orchards donates apples and cherries and cultivates rows of sweet corn and fields of cabbage for the food bank. Other local farmers that work with the food bank include Klein Orchards, Sandy Bottom Berries and the Agsearch Company. Volunteers of the food bank often visit these local farms to help with the gleaning process. Additionally, Estelle has procured vegetable plants like tomatoes and peppers from local nurseries to help redistribute to the pantries for those who may wish to grow their own vegetables. As an added measure of sustainability, Estelle ensures that no spoiled vegetables go to waste, incorporating them into feed for local animals.

The resources Estelle and his staff glean for the hungry go not only to pantries but also other emergency food relief organizations, such as Kids Food Basket. Celebrating its tenth anniversary, Kids Food Basket has been leveraging resources to send out over 4,200 sack supper meals each day to over thirty-five schools. Bridget Clarke Whitney, the organization's director, constantly reminds our community that while "poverty is complex, feeding a child is not."[64] With a simple meal that includes a sandwich, snack, fruit and/or vegetable and drink, Whitney wants to ensure that no child in Grand Rapids goes to bed hungry.

Without proper brain food, Whitney says, kids can't learn. It's also not enough to just think about the dinnertime meal. Whitney uses the sack suppers to share information with the parents and families that might help them address their own food security. "Approximately ten times a year, we include materials in the sack suppers with information on food pantries, United Way's 211, nutrition education resources and additional food security information that relates to programs such as Double-Up Food Bucks, SNAP benefits and local farmer's markets," says Whitney.

Whitney has a special love for Michigan agriculture and wants to see the local food supply chain better integrated into the Kids Food Basket program. "Recently, we created a presentation specifically targeted for the local agriculture community about Kids Food Basket and ways we can collaborate," she notes. "Specifically, we are hoping to connect with a few local farms to grow specific items for sack suppers."

Like Feeding America West Michigan, Kids Food Basket also hosts a u-pick volunteer program. Whitney notes:

> *Each spring, we create an account at several local farms and have volunteer groups head to the farms to pick pounds of fresh berries and other fruits and vegetables for sack suppers. Typically, the volunteers will return to KFB with the produce, wash it and repack it into single-serving items. This is a triple win—it's a benefit for the farmers, it's a fantastic volunteer opportunity that puts children and adults in touch with fresh produce while serving others and it provides freshly picked local produce for the kids we serve.*

MORE THAN EMERGENCY RELIEF: A SOCIAL JUSTICE REFRAME

Lisa Oliver-King of Our Kitchen Table explicitly states that when discussing the root causes of food injustice, Grand Rapids must "create a totally new framework of food justice and food sovereignty."[65] In defining food sovereignty and food justice, Oliver-King suggests focusing on government policy, land use and the capitalistic underpinnings of the current food system—including the cultural construct of food deserts, labor issues and public health issues. According to Oliver-King, to arrive at a truly fair food system "would require serious planning and a need to step back and honor a process that will make some people uncomfortable." She continues:

The Grand Rapids food system, ten to fifteen years ago, was almost exclusively dependent on the global agribusiness food system, which as we all know is highly destructive and based on profit—not everyone's right to healthy food. Those most impacted by this system are working-class people and communities of color. Lack of access to fresh food was by design, since these communities are less relevant and more expendable. Grand Rapids is in no position to have a real food system based on justice until we come to terms with the institutionalized racism in Grand Rapids, the exclusion of farm workers/migrant workers from the equation, the dominance of the profit motive in "local food" efforts and the fact that no one is really addressing the agribusiness model and its local manifestations, such as fast-food restaurants, food brokers, entities like Gordon Foods and the large grocery-store chains, which continue to sell and promote the most unhealthy food we can possibly consume.

PLANTING SEEDS AND SKILLS

Addressing these core issues is the Baxter Community Center, a faith-based community center working to bring people from the community not only to discuss food justice issues but also to learn skills that will help move them toward food independence.

Danielle Veldman is an enthusiastic leader at Baxter Community Center, and she can often be found showing visitors the center's core programming, which includes an on-site food and clothing pantry, a full commercial kitchen used for cooking classes, an on-site health clinic and a fully operational greenhouse and community garden. Veldman bubbles with enthusiasm and pride when she talks about the marketplace coordinator, Janika, who promotes the fresh fruits and vegetables that come from the garden and end up being distributed in the food-pantry line. "Janika is wonderful," says Veldman. "She is our beautiful marketplace coordinator. All of the food in the greenhouse we grow comes here to the marketplace. She is the promoter of the century, always saying, 'Here, try some of this! It's good! We grew it! It's healthy.'"[66]

Veldman is honest about the struggles to cultivate her clients' tastes and preferences for fresh fruits and vegetables. "Janika is on the ground giving us feedback," says Veldman. "She's honest about what people prefer, who

Cultivating at the Baxter Community Center greenhouse. *Photo by Jonathan Stoner.*

doesn't like arugula and if we should grow something different." Greg Nunn, the garden manager, helps adjust the planting schedule to support what is wanted in the marketplace at the point of distribution. "Arugula is one of those greens that people aren't really into here," says Nunn. "Spicy greens are not a big hit here. People really like the Swiss chard." Veldman continues, "Most people are used to iceberg lettuce and romaine. Kale, collards and cooking greens are all good. If we just give them a bag of arugula greens, people seem pretty unsure of what to do with it." In the end, however, Janika believes it is important to keep growing the fresh food and getting it into the marketplace's pantry. "It works out well," says Janika. "People really enjoy fresh produce, especially when they don't have the money to pay for it."

Baxter is unique in that it also has an on-site health clinic that offers medical, dental, vision, pediatric care and hearing services, as well as supplemental programs like WIC benefits for pregnant and nursing mothers. Baxter's physicians have been coming for over twenty years and have essentially set up second volunteer practices. "When families come, they can say, 'Dr. Addy is my doctor' not 'Who am I going to see?' Families have a relationship, and the doctors know their family histories," says Veldman, noting the importance of the consistent doctor-patient relationship, especially for neighborhood patients managing chronic health conditions. The free clinic

Canning classes at the Baxter Community Center. *Photo courtesy of Baxter Community Center.*

is an important component in establishing a baseline understanding of making healthy choices and the reason why whole foods are an important part in wellness in an underserved community. Here at the clinic, patients—especially those receiving supplemental benefits such as WIC—also learn more about fresh fruits and vegetables via cooking classes and visiting the garden and greenhouse.

Over the past decade, both messaging and benefits for those women needing WIC has evolved to include targeted education about the importance of and access to healthy fresh fruits and vegetables. Traditionally, education was based on a very conventional nutrition education program. The food pyramid was shared, and the food choices or needs of the clients (Hispanic, Asian, etc) may or may not have been taken into consideration when talking about preferences, cooking habits or lifestyles. But at Baxter, because of the additional resources of the greenhouse, garden and kitchen classes, access to information is more comprehensive. A pregnant or nursing woman can learn about healthy foods right there in the garden. She can also learn where the farmers' markets are and gain access to Double Up Food Bucks or take a cooking class in the kitchen.

Baxter's kitchen provides the space to teach the skills to use these fresh fruits and vegetables. Veldman and her team of volunteers, led by local neighborhood champions, expose the neighbors to new foods via kitchen demos, cooking classes and canning classes. Veldman notes that she tries to make these classes community focused, like the community cook-off at the fall tomato festival.

Just outside the community center, yarrow grows outside of the greenhouse alongside happy tomatoes. Onions, started in January, sit in harvest baskets, while a high school intern works diligently to string the tomatoes. Like the Treehouse Garden, neighbors walk by and holler through the fences.

Veldman believes in the power of bringing people together around food to spark conversations about food justice and to promote cultural backgrounds and identities. "This brings people together to discuss their food history and stories," she says. "It makes me excited to come to work everyday."

Chapter 8

Growing a Bumper Crop of Smart, Healthy Kids

Teaching kids how to feed themselves and how to live in a community responsibly is the center of an education.
—Alice Waters

Perhaps one of the most unfortunate results of the globalization and industrialization of the United States food system is the lack of knowledge our children have about the origins of their food. Our children no longer understand the seasons in which food is grown, as many kinds of food are always available in the local supermarket. Our children are disconnected from the environmental, social and economic impacts of the global food trade.

Because of readily available processed foods, our children have a difficult time making the connection between their health and the importance of fresh vegetables and foods as a regular part of their diet. While our food system continues in this manner, our society faces a myriad of challenges, perhaps the scariest of which is the childhood obesity epidemic. This is no longer health food fear mongering. Our children will simply not live as long due to Type 2 diabetes and other obesity-related chronic health problems caused by a poor diet and lack of exercise.

There is hope, however. In lunchrooms, gardens and around the evening dinner table, concerned adults are trying to save the lives of these children by introducing them to the soil that offers them nourishment and a place to dine and nourish their little bodies and minds.

THE LUNCH LINE

If you grew up in the '70s and '80s, you remember the Salisbury steak (mystery meat!) that was served on a tray by a real lunch lady. Back then, many schools still had in-house cooks on staff and prepared their meals in full-service commercial kitchens. In the '90s, many schools facing budget shortfalls resorted to bringing off-site contractors to the schools to provide the lunches, including many fast-food establishments such as Pizza Hut and Taco Bell, while trying to increase revenue for extracurricular activities by signing on exclusive contracts with soda companies like Coca-Cola and Pepsi.

In light of the childhood obesity epidemic and the growing trend toward local food, teachers, parents and administrators in schools around the country are trying to change what's in their lunch lines. In schools, administrators are designing food service teams focused on a core mission to make sure each and every child is at his or her academic best by being well nourished and ready to learn.

In Grand Rapids, the first organized school lunch was served at Central School in 1902. At the time, Central School served a large area of the city, and many students could not go home for lunch. An experimental program served forty to fifty students at a lunch counter. First come, first served was the rule, and that menu from 1903 included roast veal and potato salad. Times have changed, and nearly 110 years later, the Grand Rapids Public Schools (GRPS) system has seen its share of challenges but remains committed to its original 1902 goal—serving a hot meal for both breakfast and lunch to children who need to eat so that they can learn in the classroom.[67]

Today, Grand Rapids Public Schools serves approximately twenty-two thousand meals a day to students in its own district and also serves as a contract food service provider to the more affluent neighboring school district of East Grand Rapids. GRPS, like many public school systems across the country, takes part in the federal National School Lunch Program.

At the helm of the largest school-food service department is a man over six feet tall, reminiscent of Paul Bunyan. Towering in presence but gentle in spirit, Paul Baumgartner is the director of Grand Rapids Public Schools' Food and Nutrition Services Department. But don't confuse him for the lunch lady—Baumgartner prefers to be called the "Food Dude." Photos in his office portray a variety of hobbies, boat building among them, as well as a 1970s photo featuring a teenaged Baumgartner helping construct the large barn on the Milo Farm at the Blandford Nature Center. "I would take the crosstown bus to Blandford. I was in their first class of sixth graders in 1973," he recalls.[68]

From there, Baumgartner went on to graduate from City High School and then attended Michigan State, earning a degree in hotel, restaurant and institutional management. "The industry has definitely changed since I received my degree," says Baumgartner. "I've worked in institutional food service at Steelcase and Kent County Hospital and have been at Grand Rapids Public Schools since 1989. We continue to get better at our jobs for our kids every year."

At a time when most school districts have dismantled their prep kitchens and farmed out their lunch preparation to corporate food service providers and even fast-food companies, Grand Rapids Public Schools is serving daily made-from-scratch meals prepared in a real, centralized kitchen. Here, the staff has the ability to exercise quality control over food procurement, including local foods. "We are getting the word out about our efforts in purchasing local foods, but there are also trade-offs," explains Baumgartner. "There are budget issues and the challenge of working on the scale that we do. Every day, staff members fill the kitchen to prepare meals from scratch. They prepare about seven thousand breakfasts for kids each day, about thirteen thousand lunches and then another two thousand after-school snacks. To put that in some kind of perspective, we have to have twenty-five—that's right, twenty-five—fifty-five-gallon drums of milk available every day."

The department orders foods directly from farmers as well as other local produce distributors such as Van Eerden's whenever possible. Traceability is important. "The supply chain is getting better, and we are improving our local purchasing in a variety of ways," explains Baumgartner. "We are asking our suppliers to provide us with QR codes. There are [produce] packinghouses all over West Michigan. I am working with them to help identify where the food is coming from—whether the farm is in Salinas, California, or Hudsonville, Michigan. Knowing about that farm is important, especially if the farm is a place where our kids' families might work."

From local bread to milk, cheese, apples and asparagus, GRPS is demonstrating that it is working to make change and buy locally to the degree that it can. "In October, for example, we focus on apples and winter squash on the menus," explains Baumgartner. "We partner with dietetics interns who help the students taste different foods—all different kinds of roasted squash with different toppings. And then we go from there and tweak the menu so the kids can see the input they gave."

For Baumgartner, food is brain fuel. "It is the cornerstone for making sure that your child can perform academically," he says. "New USDA regulations have higher emphasis on fresh fruit and vegetables, whole grains, beans and less sodium. We are right in line with what they are asking for. We don't need to try to get our kids used to whole grains or eating new fresh fruits and vegetables. Red beans and rice? We've being doing that for a long time."

GRPS' menus not only reflect seasonality but also the cultures of the students in the buildings, with traditional foods on the menu like red beans and rice and black-eyed peas. They are also introducing new foods to the students, including roasted local squashes, purple power salads with cucumbers and red and green pepper strips. Baumgartner notes:

> We take the time to talk about why we should eat these foods. The servers, cooks, lunch staff—they're all are here to support the meal. Their presence and attitude makes a difference as to whether the kid takes an extra taste of food or trashes it. Repeat messaging is also important. Repeat, repeat, repeat. It's a lifelong process to encourage healthy habits. It's crucial to message the importance of these same meals—we need to reach the parents. It's not enough to have a pizza party, so we are serving the school meals at parents' night. We want to show them quality and also have them understand the importance of healthy meals at home.

Baumgartner recruits registered dietician (RD) interns to support their work and also partners with agencies such as the Michigan State University Extension to make community connections around children's health, particularly in the area of obesity, fitness and healthy eating habits. "RDs are a wonderful resource—we want them to get excited about school meals," notes Baumgartner. "Having them develop an understanding of school meals and how meal programs work is critical for their future, whether they work in a clinic or independently."

However, there are limits to Baumgartner's reach. "Some schools use food as a reward—not all schools believe food is fuel," he acknowledges. "It really boils down to the building's principal, the PTO and the parents at the building level." While GRPS doesn't have a mandated district-wide food policy to address sales of snacks, sodas and foods in the classroom, Baumgartner's team is ready to help teachers make classroom connections. "A teacher can have a lot of fun with the information we give them about the food," says Baumgartner. "Everything and anything can be related to the meal—social studies programs, math, etc. It depends on the teacher and school and their creativity. We can support these things academically by sharing the knowledge base and getting resources to the teachers."

Bringing the Classroom into the Garden

In today's educational environment, most children's learning experiences are determined by a need to meet standardized learning guidelines and limited by an ever-increasing focus on performance. Fortunately, there are teachers willing to go the extra mile and schools designed around the idea that kids should get outside, get dirty and learn by doing. One of these teachers is Holly Orions, outdoor educator at the West Michigan Academy for Environmental Sciences. Located just outside downtown Grand Rapids, Orions's classroom is the outdoors. The acreage surrounding the school is home to a variety of ecosystems that she uses for teaching, including a wetlands area, woods, a bit of prairie and a cultivated community garden complete with a greenhouse, chickens and a mud oven.

Orions has spent nearly nine years cultivating this dream outdoor education space, relying on the magic of the natural world around her to get kids to connect to the Earth and open up. "One of the first struggles with incorporating the environment into the everyday school day is making sure that students feel comfortable in the outdoors and comfortable in the place where they are learning," explains Orions. "I use what nature has to offer and go from there."[69] The kids' reactions keep Orions going. "They say things like, 'This is the best dirt I've ever eaten' after munching on a carrot right out of the ground and 'I could eat beets for every meal' and 'Can you teach my mom how to cook vegetables?' It doesn't seem to matter the age; they all have grown to be fond of this place and see at as part of themselves. It is an awesome thing to witness—the connection that forms from knowing your place."

Orions and her students grow over 30 percent of what they eat in their salad bar. "From September to December and March to June, we have spinach and salad greens from our hoop house," says Orions. "The students love the salad bar and clean it out—every last bit of lettuce and carrot gone! That is the sign of success. And the food-service department is supportive of using fresh, school-grown food."

Orions believes this type of garden-based nutrition education makes permanent changes with kids and their eating habits, noting:

> *My kids are really proud of themselves when they bring a healthy snack or make a recipe at home that we've done in class. I see a lot of changes. In the past nine years at the school, I have witnessed a shift in food that is brought in by the students and what is served in the cafeteria and at snack time. I attribute that to the school community being excited not just about food but healthy food.*

Parents are also noticing the changes and asking Orions what they can do to keep the changes happening at home:

> *I say, "If they grow it, they will eat it." The parents are always shocked and at first seemed scared to garden or try new things. But as the years have gone by and their kids have gotten older, they are embracing this way of eating and are now asking about seed catalogs, and we even exchange seeds and plants! Many times, inner-city kids are limited in their food choices because of proximity to grocery stores, reliance upon public transportation and lack of parental support. In order to stop a cycle of poor nutrition, obesity, behavior issues, etc, kids need to learn where their food comes from and how it's grown so that they can get out there and make their own choices.*

Orions recognizes the efforts that this sort of education takes but says it's important to persevere because the rewards are great. "Be willing to put the time in to see the outcome, because it works," she says. "We have seen a rise in science scores on the standardized tests over the past eight years, student behavior has improved and attitudes about health and wellness have changed." Orions assures teachers, "Edible education needs to be given time to grow, and when it is ripe and ready, the outcomes are amazing. All the hard work pays off, and in the end, the kids are the ones who are given the rewards." She extends similar encouragement to parents, recognizing the importance of integrating healthy behaviors into the home: "Look at it as a way to learn to solve problems as a family, to spend time together, learn together and, ultimately, share food together."

Epilogue

Sowing Hope for the Future

B ack at the Treehouse Community Garden, Amy Bowditch talks more
about the purpose behind the local food revolution: "All we want to do
is grow food…show them there is a life outside of prepackaged food. It's so
much more than the food—it isn't about the food. This builds hope."

She notes that the garden was designed to be a sanctuary. "We have a
lot of violence in this immediate neighborhood and even on this street,"
says Bowditch. "My house has been shot at four times. I have bullet holes
in my stove. It's really dangerous. It's usually bustling with a gang. We see
the yelling, the screaming, the domestic abuse and kids being neglected. It's
really hard."

Amy's tone changes when turning back to the garden. "We have five
families growing here now. Not bad for our first year," she says with a smile.
"We had one neighbor talking to another who said, 'I'm just going to wait till
next year to see what happens.' The reply from another gardener was pretty
awesome. She said, 'If you wait, nothing's going to happen.' I thought that
was good advice."

Bowditch describes the times over the summer when the neighbors came
together. She reminisces about the mud pit that came out of the construction
area in the spring when the rains came while they were building the beds.

She reflects on how the garden space gives them respite from the harshness of their day-to-day lives and allows them the space to laugh and to play:

Kids don't have that sense of play in a city environment. We wanted to have a space where the kids feel welcome. It's kind of like a barrier from the rest of the world. It's a tiny barrier, but it's something. The kids are so stressed out from their home lives, but they don't event know how to articulate that they are stressed out. It surfaces in their relationships and how they treat each other. When they are here, we can see that something is happening on a deeper level. I can't even imagine how helpful that is and is going to be in their future. And I want to keep gardening with the kids. This changes their lives forever. It gives them so much more than just an experience in the natural world—it gives them a sense of responsibility, a sense of purpose. If you give a kid a plant, they take care of it—but they also learn what happens if you don't take care of it. I feel like it's a way to instill in them a spark of hope in their lives because there is so much here that beats them down daily.

There are some technical learning curves being faced by the new gardeners. "We appreciate the support of the Baxter Community Center," says Bowditch. "We get a lot of plants from them, and we can use their greenhouse in the winter." She then points over to the Cooper's family garden plot, which in the middle of the summer is a bit overrun with vegetables. "This is the thing we are trying to teach—thinning and spacing," she says. "This is everyone's learning curve. But it's fun to watch plants. It's crazy to see how fast things grow." Bowditch contemplates the future of the community garden space:

I would like to see it become a place where the neighbors are investing their time. We have such a small space compared to other community gardens, but it's perfect for our block. We aren't trying to reach a large scale. Certainly people can come from anywhere, but we want the neighbors to enjoy this. We want it to be their garden.

Beyond that? I don't know. I think that is the enjoyment...that we have of these dreams. We just start in one place and keep moving forward, which is exciting because people's needs change...the neighborhood changes. I like that space to be open—it leaves room for creativity.

Let's keep the master plan in the shed.

Notes

1. Amy Bowditch, Treehouse Community Garden. Interview and discussion with the author. July 2012.
2. Elissa Sangalli Hillary, Local First. Interview and discussion with the author. February 5, 2013.
3. Tyler Dornbos, The Salon. Interview and discussion with the author. July 13, 2012.
4. Suzanne Schultz, Grand Rapids city planner. Interview and discussion with the author. July 17, 2012.
5. Tom Cary, Groundswell Farm. Interview and discussion with the author. January 17, 2013.
6. Cynthia Price, Grand Rapids Food Systems Council. Interview and discussion with the author. January 24, 2013.
7. Michigan Environmental Council. http://www.environmentalcouncil. org/priorities/article.php?x=114.
8. Holly Bechiri, local food advocate. Personal correspondence. July 8, 2010
9. Anne Guilfoyle, Grand Rapids citizen. Letter to Grand Rapids City Commission. July 12, 2010
10. Herbruck's Poultry Ranch. Presentation to Grand Rapids City Commission. July 2010.
11. Stephanie Pierce, Farmer. Letter to Grand Rapids City Commission. August 4, 2010.
12. Suzanne Schultz, Grand Rapids city planner. Interview and discussion with the author. July 16, 2012.

13. Andy Dragt, Uptown Farm. Interview and discussion with the author. July 2012.

14. Andy Dragt, Uptown Farm. Interview and discussion with the author. September 2012.

15. Lisa Oliver-King, Our Kitchen Table. Interview and discussion with the author. February 25, 2013.

16. Bing Goei, Eastern Floral. Interview and discussion with the author. October 11, 2012.

17. Ibid.

18. Bing Goei, Bethany Christian Services. Interview and discussion with the author. September 2012.

19. United States Department of Agriculture. http://www.agcensus. usda.gov/Publications/2007/Online_Highlights/County_Profiles/ Michigan/cp26081.pdf.

20. Karen Lubbers, Lubbers Farm. Interview and discussion with the author. October 22, 2012.

21. Rachel Hood, West Michigan Environmental Action Council. Interview and discussion with the author. February 7, 2013.

22. Michael VanderBrug, Trillium Haven Farm. Interview and discussion with the author. February 2013.

23. Tom Cary, Groundswell Farm. Interview and discussion with the author. January 17, 2013.

24. Ben Bylsma, Real Food Farms. Interview and discussion with the author. August 1, 2012.

25. San Chez Twentieth Anniversary advertisement. Fall 2012.

26. Greg Gilmore, The Gilmore Collection. Interview and discussion with the author. February 7, 2013.

27. Patrick Wise, The Essence Restaurant Group. Interview and discussion with the author. August 13, 2012.

28. Matthew Russell, Bartertown Diner and Wednesday Evening Cookies. Interview and discussion with the author. January 2013.

29. George Aquino, Restaurant reviewer. Interview and discussion with the author. January 2, 2013.

30. Tory O'Haire, The Starving Artist. Interview and discussion with the author. December 2012.

31. Kelly LeCoy, Uptown Kitchen. Interview and discussion with the author. July 17, 2012.

32. Amy Ruis, Art of the Table. Interview and discussion with the author. November 27, 2012.

33. Nicolas Mika, Entrepreneur. Interview and discussion with the author. May 22, 2012.

34. Lysandra and Aliyah French, Rochelle's A Little Something Sweet. Interview and discussion with the author. July 2012.

35. Molly Clauhs, Grand Rapids Cooking School. November 27, 2012.

36. Leigh Vandermolen, Kava House. Interview and discussion with the author. October 26, 2012.

37. Chad Morton, Direct Trade Coffee Club. Interview and discussion with the author. September 24, 2012.

38. Ryan Knapp, Madcap. Interview and discussion with the author. April 2010.

39. Trevor Corlett, Madcap. Interview and discussion with the author. April 2010.

40. Kurt Stauffer, Rowster. Interview and discussion with the author. June 2012.

41. Dave Engbers, Founders Brewing Co. Interview and discussion with the author. February 4, 2013.

42. Michelle Sellers, BarFly Ventures. Interview and discussion with the author. February 11, 2013.

43. Z.Z. Lydens, *The Story of Grand Rapids*. Grand Rapids, MI: Kregel Publications, 1966. 296–97.

44. Ibid.

45. Ibid.

46. Tyler Nickerson, local brewer. Interview and discussion with the author. January 2013.

47. Amy Sherman, Great American Brew Trail. Interview and discussion with the author. November 1, 2012.

48. Andy Sietsema, Sietsema Orchards. Interview and discussion with the author. October 18, 2012.

49. Weston Eaton, "Is Craft Beer a Social Movement?" http://sicilianosmkt. blogspot.com/2013/02/is-craft-beer-social-movement.html.

50. Ibid.

51. Christine Helms-Maletic, Fulton Street Farmers' Market. Interview and discussion with the author. September 17, 2012.

52. Jon Nunn, Grand Action. Interview and discussion with the author. September 2012.

53. Lisa Oliver-King, Our Kitchen Table. Interview and discussion with the author. February 25, 2013.

54. Julie Sielawa, YMCA of Greater Grand Rapids. January 23, 2013.

55. Sarah Chartier, Spectrum Health Hospitals. Interview and discussion with the author. February 19, 2013.

56. John Russo. Carrettino Italian Market & Wine. Interview and discussion with the author. March 8, 2013.

57. Elijah Brumback, "Food Follies: Economics, Perceptions Work Against Attracting Downtown Grocery." MiBiz, March 4, 2013.

58. Kendra Wills, "Several 'Healthy Corner Stores' in Grand Rapids Ready to Expand," Michigan State University Extension. March 8, 2013.

59. Sherri Rop, Nourish Organic Market. Interview and discussion with the author. February 4, 2013.

60. Holly Bechiri, "Joel Salatin Reflects on City Life, Kitchen Time and the Grand Rapids Chicken Fight." *The Rapidian*, January 19, 2012.

61. Barb Duchemin, Temple Emanuel. Interview and discussion with the author. October 2012.

62. Feeding America West Michigan, Quarterly newsletter, www.feedingamericawestmichigan.org. Fall 2012.

63. Ken Estelle. Director, Feeding America West Michigan. Interview and discussion with the author. August 10, 2012.

64. Bridget Clark Whitney. Director, Kids Food Basket. Interview and discussion with the author. January 24, 2013.

65. Lisa Oliver-King, Our Kitchen Table. Interview and discussion with the author. February 25, 2013.

66. Danielle Veldman, Baxter Community Center. Interview and discussion with the author. June 25, 2012.

67. Matt Gladden, "WYCE's Glance at the Past: School Lunches." http://archive.org/details/GlanceAtThePast-SchoolLunches.

68. Paul Baumgartner, Director of Food Nutrition Services. Grand Rapids Public Schools. Interview and discussion with the author. October 18, 2012.

69. Holly Orions, West Michigan Academy of Environmental Sciences. Interview and discussion with the author. November 2012.

About the Author

With a background in anthropology and a professional focus on community health, Lisa Rose Starner has gathered her food and farming knowledge from many people and places along a very delicious journey over the years.

Starner grew up in Spring Lake, Michigan, just several minutes from the magical shoreline of the Big Lake. A child of the '80s, Starner was raised on a hodgepodge of foods—from home-cooked meals made with vegetables from her mother's garden to those 1980s-style frozen pot-pie dinners. Starner's mother was frugal with her food budget out of necessity, taught her family how to garden and preserve seasonal produce and worked to get her family to sit at

Photo by Adam Bird.

the dining table nearly every evening for dinner. For this, Starner remains forever grateful.

A self-taught home chef, Starner first learned the art of eating while a university student in Nice, France. After university, Starner's edible journey took her to work in the Stag's Leap District of Napa Valley and to volunteer at Alice Waters's Edible Schoolyard in Berkeley, California. It was at the Edible Schoolyard where Starner witnessed the power of growing gardens with children and the impact it can have on their health, the environment and the future of our global food system.

Starner returned to Michigan from the Bay Area in 2001. She has since been an activist in her local food community, writing, teaching and getting her own hands dirty in the soil to help grow the movement with her family in Grand Rapids. When Starner is not in her gardens or kitchen, she can be found in the fields and forests, learning from the wild plants growing in her own Great Lakes bioregion and honing her skills as an herbalist.